ROBERT WHITMAN

ROBERT WHITMAN

TURNING

SEPTEMBER 7 – 29, 2007

PACEWILDENSTEIN

534 WEST 25TH STREET NEW YORK NY 10001

TURNING

A conversation between Coosje van Bruggen and Robert Whitman

In *The American Moon*, performed late November and into December of 1960 at the Reuben Gallery, Whitman used projections of images taken outdoors that were echoed indoors during the performance. The photograph shows the audience seated in one of six tunnels around an open central space just after an 8mm film projection on a plastic curtain with paper rectangles glued to it hanging in the opening of the tunnel.

The curtain has been pulled up, but as the projector has not yet been turned off, it shines its light through the performance area into another tunnel, making the audience the movie.

Moon, 2006, plastic hemisphere with looped digital video projection, 5 feet diameter
Collection Lisa and Richard Baker, Greenwich, Connecticut

Coosje van Bruggen: Bob, you said once in a statement about your early performances that you intended them to be "...stories of a physical experience and realistic descriptions of the physical world. Description is done in terms of experience... if somebody says something is red, then everybody knows what that means because they have seen it." Does this approach underlie your attraction to the theme of the moon, the only natural satellite of the earth?

Robert Whitman: I thought it was terrific to use the NASA material that nobody had ever seen before. Our generation is the first bunch of people that actually know the moon close-up.

On the one hand that's kind of wonderful and on the other it adds another area of stuff that we can't imagine. It's just another diving board to jump off of into the unknown.

CVB: Are each of the images of the moons projected within a hemisphere?

RW: In these works the various projections from NASA and the Yohkoh satellite are wrapped around a sphere to make the movie that I used. Most of these movies are projected within a hemisphere. At least one is on a split fabric that moves with the air.

We used a database that's available from NASA. You can buy 15-discs worth of files of the moon; if you wanted to you could probably build an exact same-size model of the moon. Well, that may be an exaggeration. The resolution is a pixel per meter, and an enormous amount of actual information.

Evan Raskob, who I had met through some people at the NYU Interactive Telecommunications Program, where I had been working on *Local Report*, 2005, a project with video cell phones, downloaded the information and wrapped it around a sphere. We had several meetings to discuss various ways to animate the moons. I might ask for example, "Can you turn the moon into the sun? Can you have an eclipse? Can we have the jiggle-y, vibration-y stuff? Can we change the color of the sun? Can we change the color of the moon?"

CVB: In observing hues gradually dissolving one into another, associations such as 'Why does the moon turn green?' emerge. The moon literally getting red evokes the Luna Rossa, as described in traditional Neapolitan songs, not to speak of "once in a Blue Moon," an experience that can be traced to the moon taking on a purplish-blue hue after major volcanic eruptions.

RW: However, none of the changing colors in the four moons, earth, and sun projections are really based on nature... it is just an idea: "Let's turn it red. Let's turn it yellow. Let's turn it blue."

CVB: In your color schemes for these projections you use almost an abstract set of rules of more-or-less primary colors that you made for yourself already in your piece *Shower*, 1963, or, for instance in the performance of the same year, *Flower*, with its red flower, green cloth vines, multi-colored rags, and blue and red, red and yellow, yellow and blue lights.

RW: The color of the original images of *Europa*, *Io*, and *Ganymede* from NASA were probably generated by the way they photographed the moons through some sort of filtration system that picks out certain light waves, sometimes with bizarre colors as a result, some of which I would not even know how to name. In the future those methods will have altered... for now we're all stuck in a temporal environment that's definitely going to look unique later on.

Cover of the announcement for *The American Moon*, 1960.

In *Flower*, performed during the spring of 1963, the audience seated on both sides of the space, which was about 23 feet wide, was very near the action.

Red lights hanging in the center of the space illuminate all sides of four white muslin walls that had descended to surround the audience. After a minute or so they are replaced by yellow lights, followed by blue lights.

CVB: So on the one hand the information data in the images you applied to the diverse moon projections, the earth and the sun are rather accurate and complete, but on the other hand, those applied to the motions are not?

RW: In *Io*, we tumbled the stuff and made it bigger and smaller, that's all. So it zooms in and zooms out very slowly and of course the image will be fragmented a little bit and be changed spatially by the cloth material that it's going to be projected on. If you would look at an apple for instance, by zooming in and out, it would all of a sudden turn into a planet or a universe. A similar organic process takes place in *Io*. The hemisphere of *Moon* is five feet across and the image is rear-projected from within. The moon rotates in relation to other astral bodies, but not in relation to the earth because the same side is always facing the earth. In the piece there is not a realistic tumble, more a kind of spinning and rotating on two axes. As time passes the rotation slows down and reverses.

The color changes and the motions of the moons are really abstract ways of measuring time, marking time, which is the major point.

CVB: When you first started to do these continuous projections without an actual beginning or end, how did you arrive at the duration of each piece? Do you rely on your own experience or do you have a kind of standard measure of how much time should pass?

RW: Between 12 and 20 minutes is about the right time to be repetitive and meditative at the same time. There's a question of how much boredom you can stand: when you're looking, you don't want to know how it is going to turn out. You want to have an adventure for your mind. I like surprises.

Usually the movements, simple axes of rotation, rumbling, and spinning are pretty slow, but in *Moon* the speed increases all of a sudden, causing a dizzying effect, and one realizes that a chunk of time and another chunk has passed. It has become a way to mark time.

CVB: As the technology of the earth, sun and moon projections does not interest you as much as achieving your aesthetics, Evan may propose something to you, you may not know immediately how to fit in, and so trigger your imagination. Not unlike how you related to performers in *The American Moon*. For instance you were prepared to transform the Reuben Gallery into your own space viscerally and psychologically. You had some specific notes and pencil sketches ready in advance but would not fix certain sequences. You were precise in selecting your performers, often dancers and artists themselves, whom you could count on because they understood your work. At the same time others participated from whom you tended to get a random feedback. In not knowing exactly their reactions, you took advantage of the occurrence of chance elements which enlivened the actions you set out to do.

RW: These kind of collaborations happen only within a certain set of understood rules. This is the way Evan and I worked on the movies.

CVB: Are such additional random effects present in the *Moon* installation outdoors at the Baker family's home?

RW: The first time I went to see that installation of *Moon*, which is outdoors in a tree, it looked like it actually was moving between the branches Not exactly random, but maybe unexpected. I like setting up possibilities without having expectations of the effect of the work.

CVB: How did you orchestrate the viewing of *Moon* at the Baker's?

RW: Mainly it has to be dark out, nighttime. I set it up so that the projection can be turned on from the house. The moon in the tree is visible both from the family's house and from another building on the property.

CVB: Will the interaction of the different sun, earth and moon projections automatically absorb the conditions of the indoor gallery space and will they determine how to move through a spatio-temporal experience just like in your performances?

RW: That would be nice.

Sun, 2007, installed on the roof of PaceWildenstein, as viewed from 11th Avenue and 22nd Street.

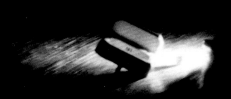

In many of Whitman's performances, fact and fiction interact through the use of live action and film projections. In *Light Touch*, first performed in 1976, actual things seemed less true to themselves than their ethereal ghosts. A projection of a cinderblock floated in the back of a truck that had been backed into the depot. Then a real cinderblock was unloaded from the truck.

The large doorway remained open so that the audience could look out into the street. A piece of fabric hung in the doorway functioned as a screen for another projection of a brown paper bag starting out small and getting larger and larger; a hand around a light bulb also appeared and changed size on the fabric screen. From time to time the cloth was blown aside by a gust of wind and the street scene of trucks and cars passing by merged with the event.

S U N

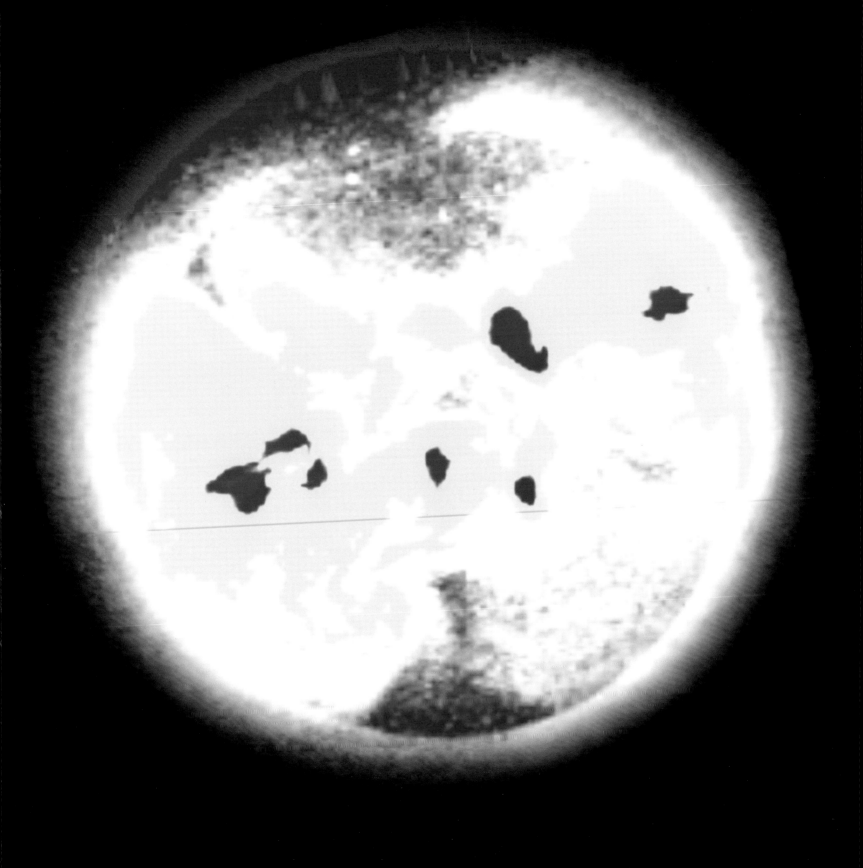

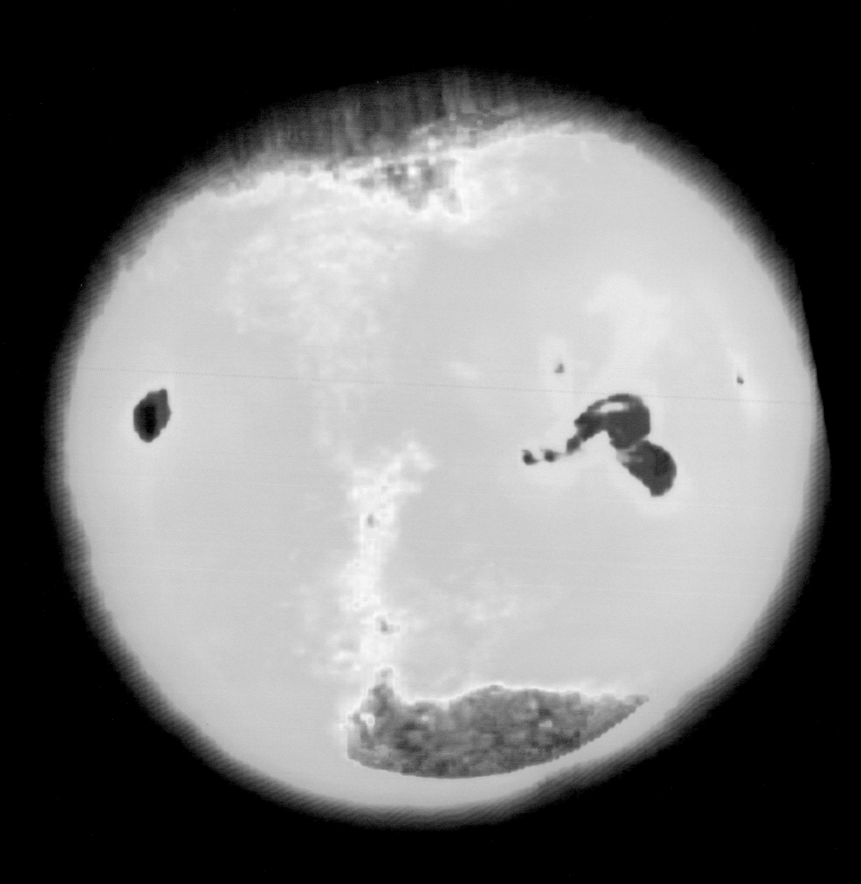

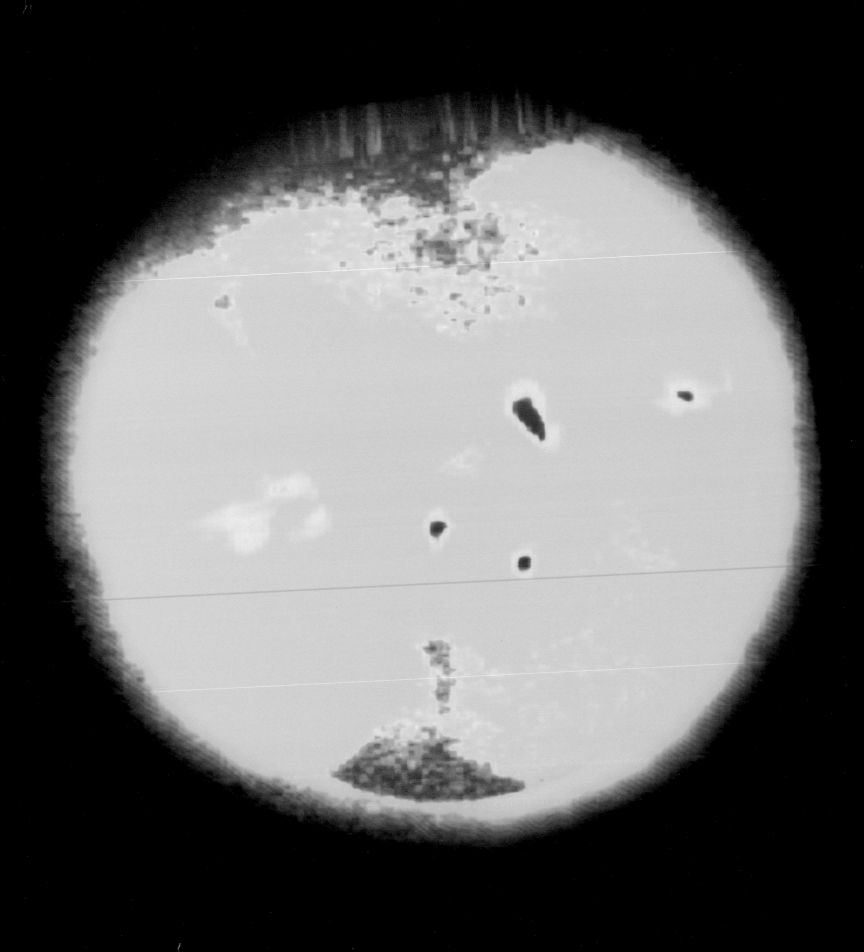

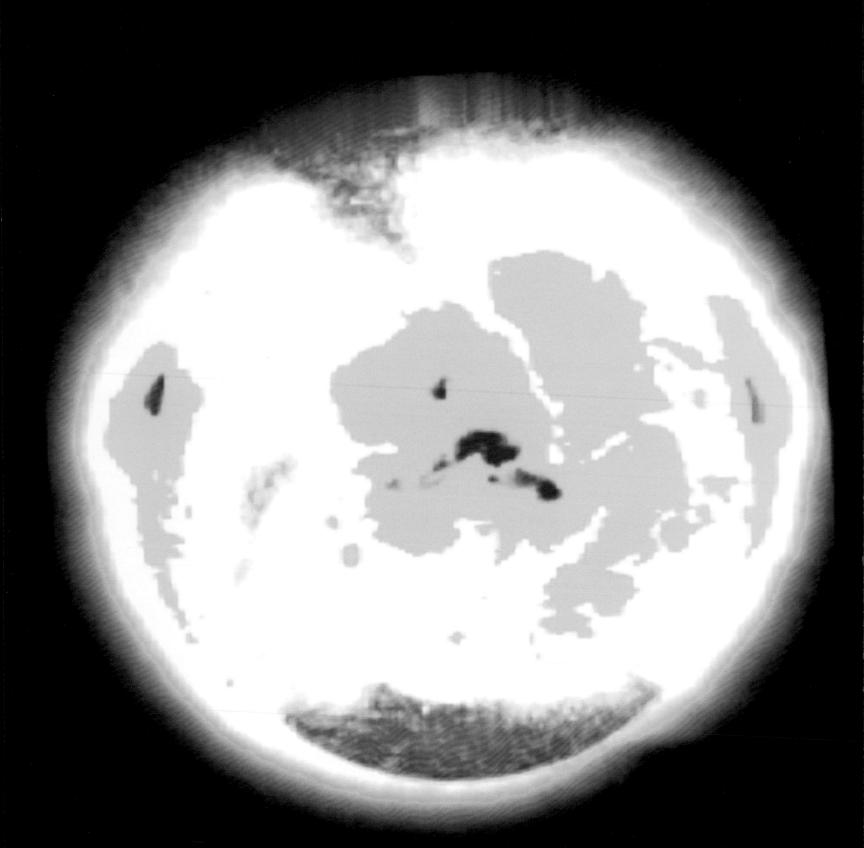

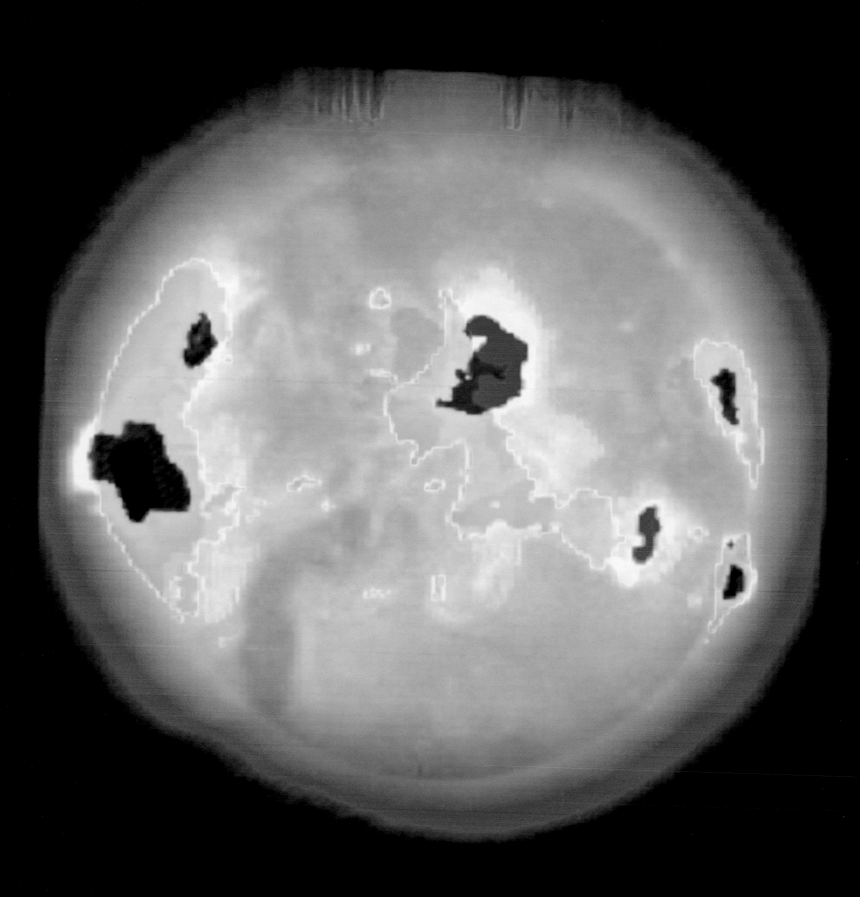

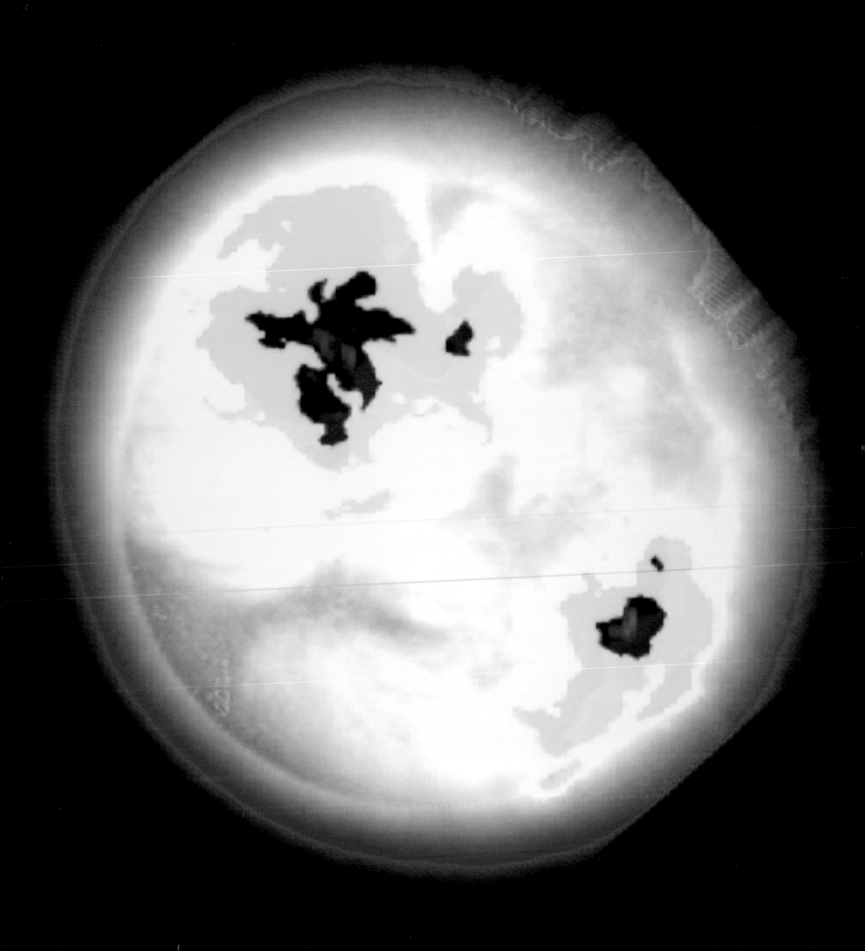

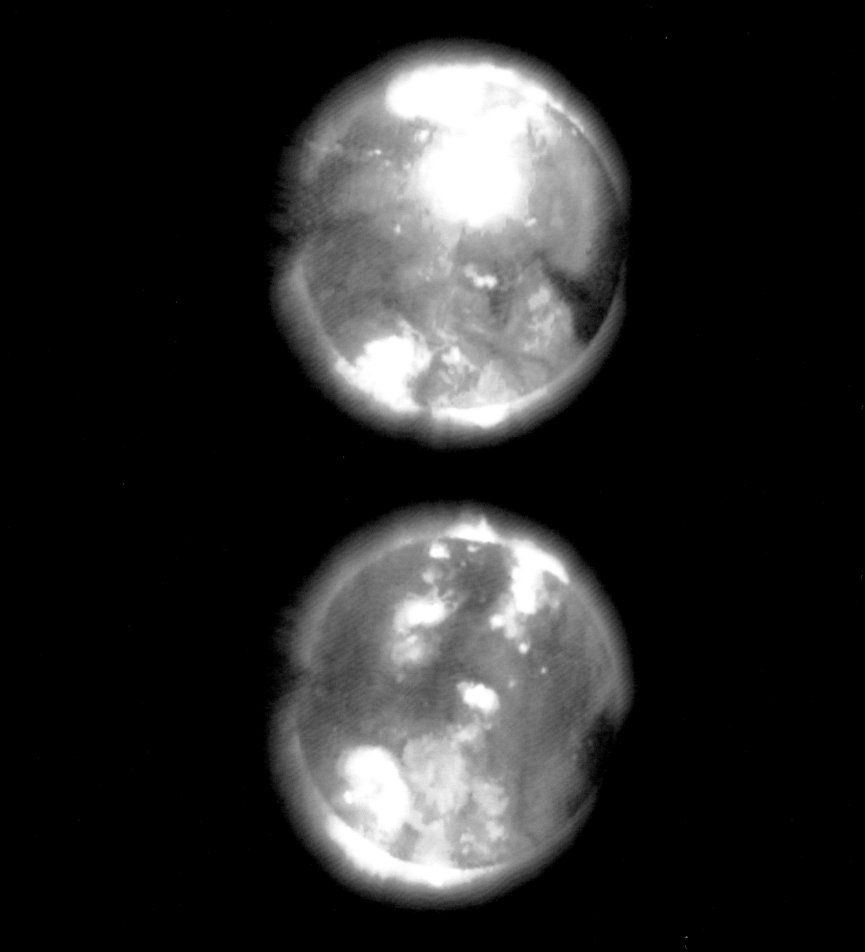

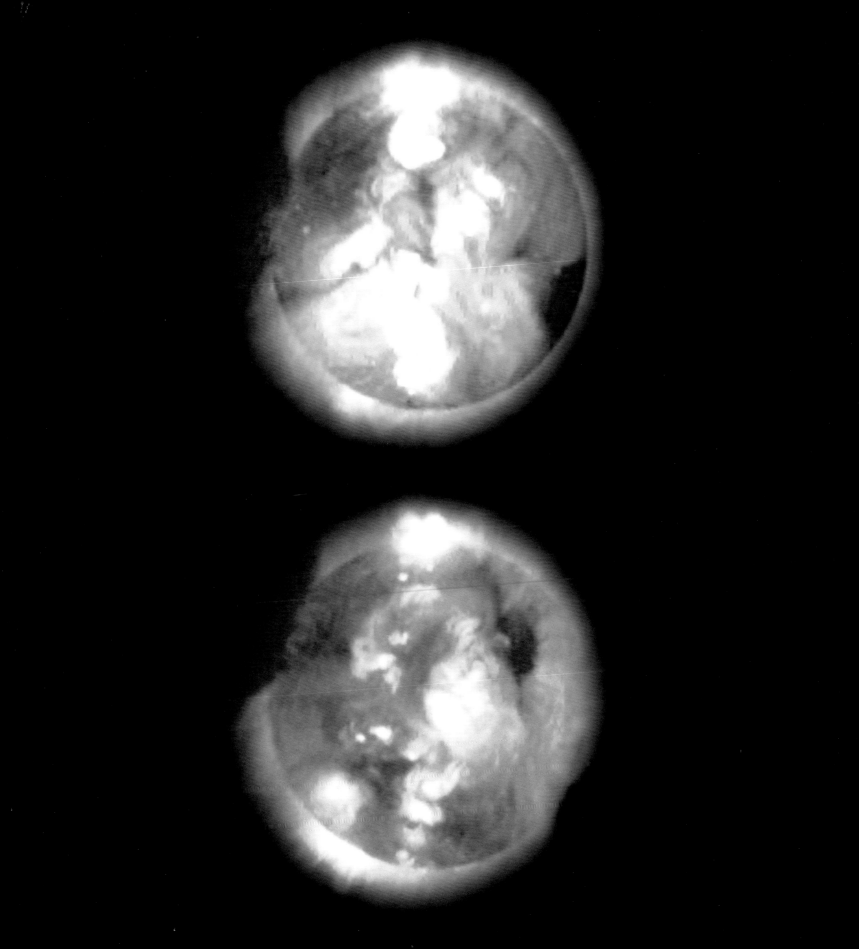

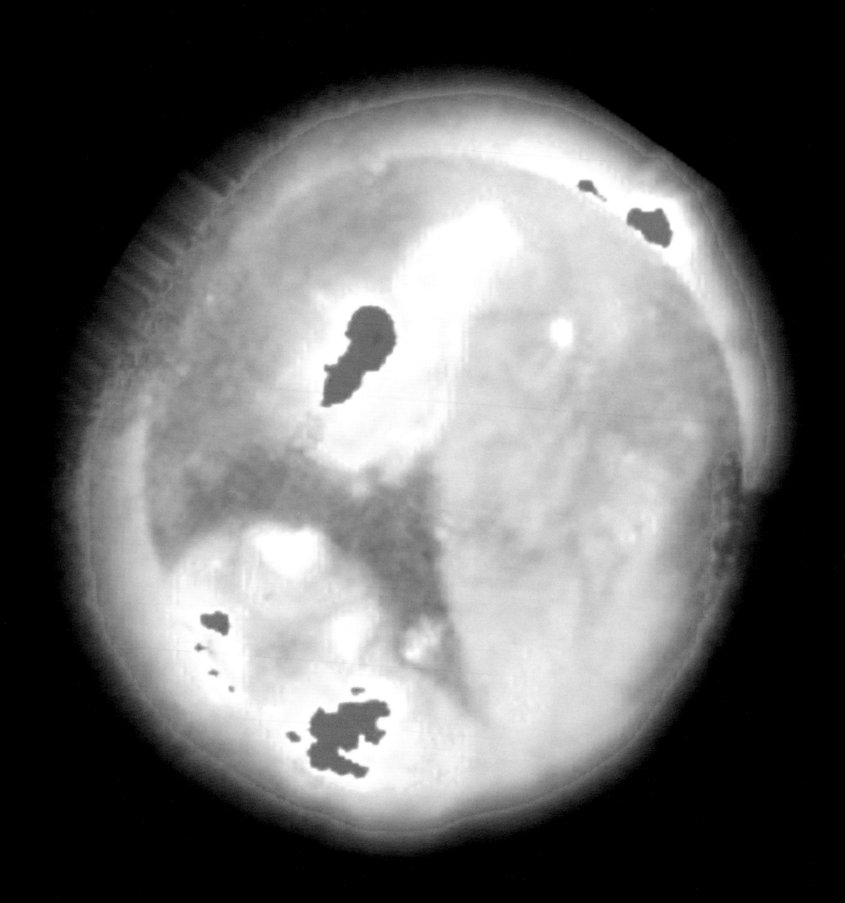

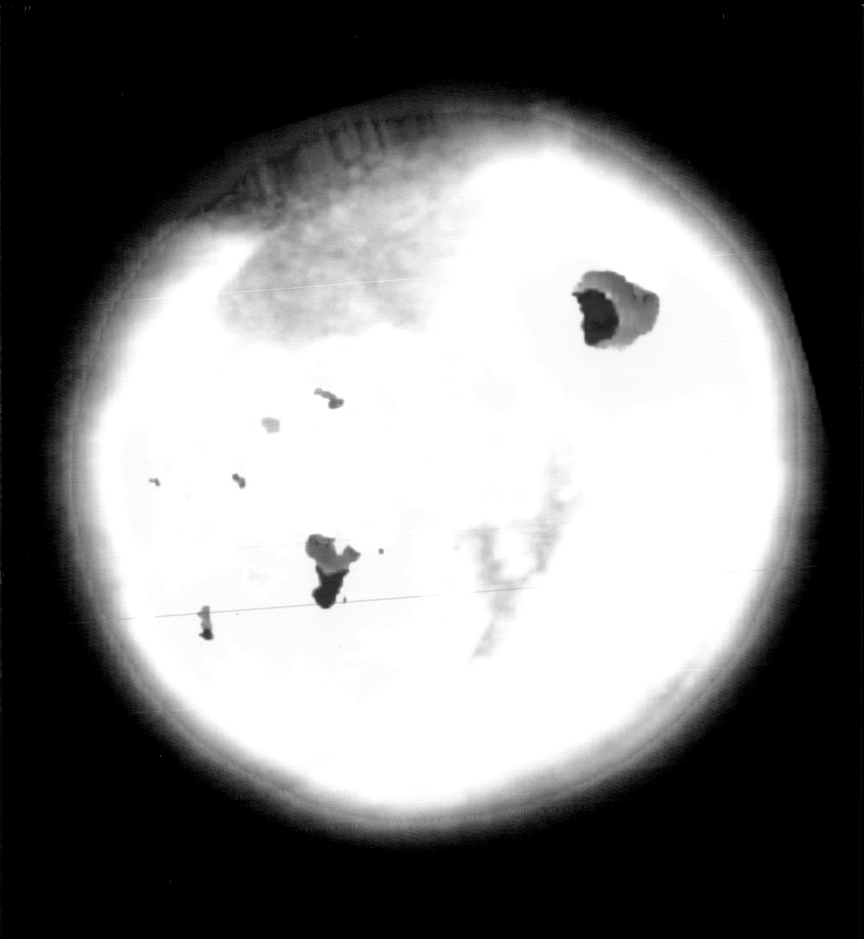

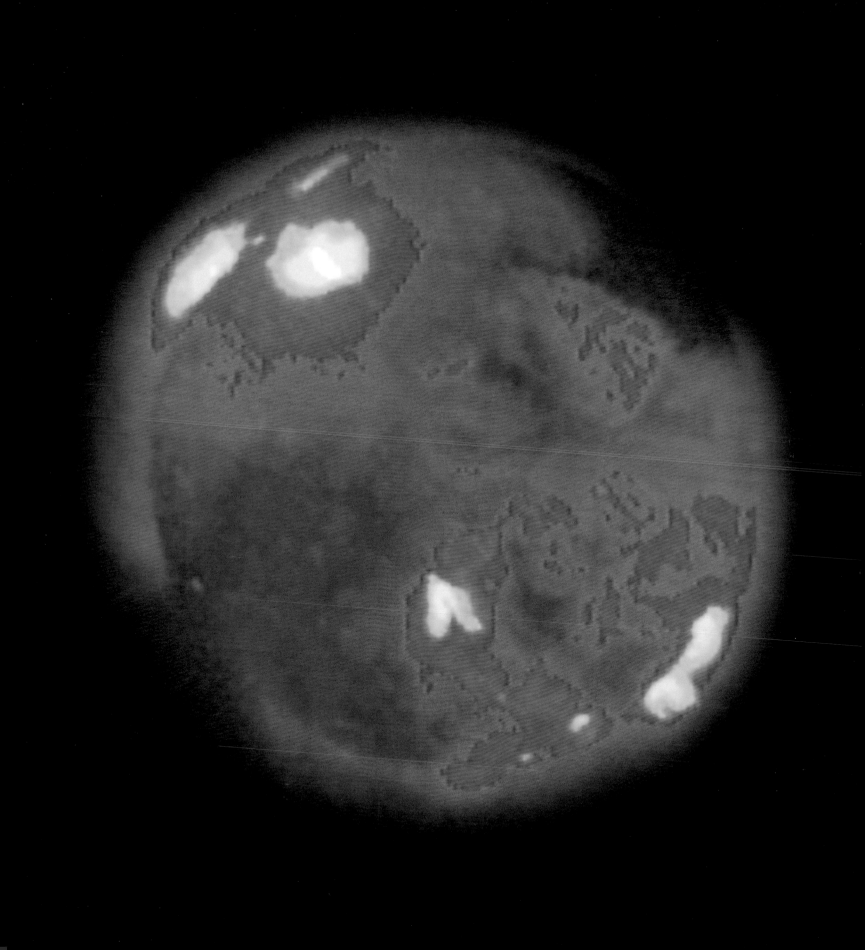

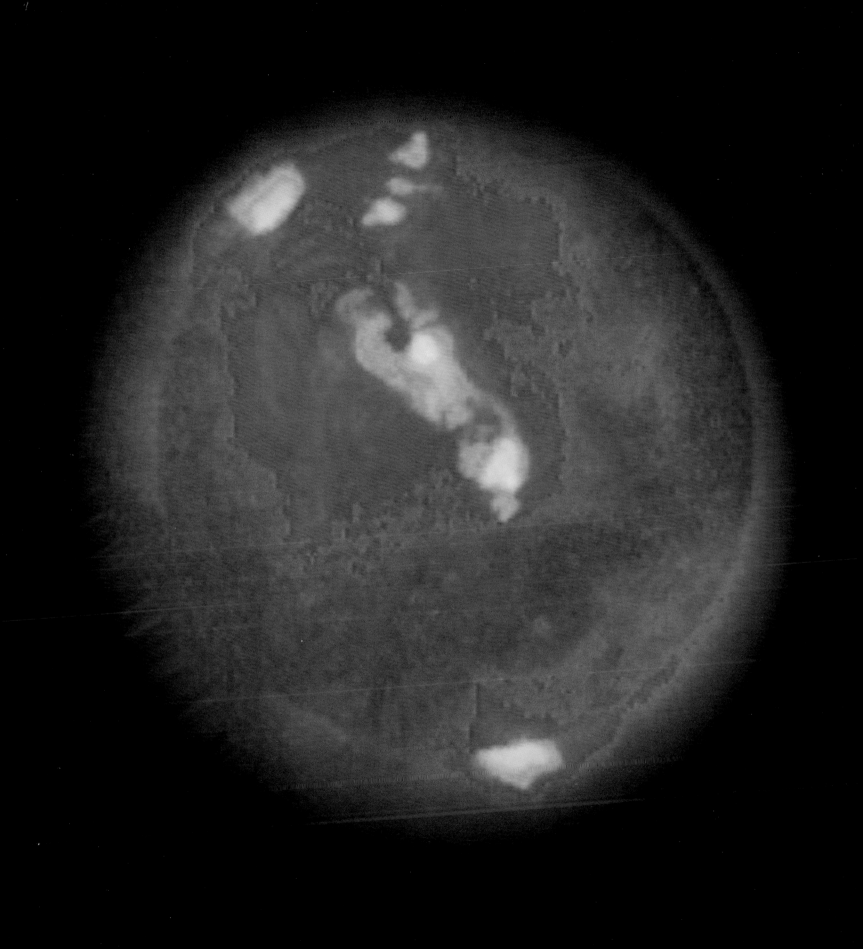

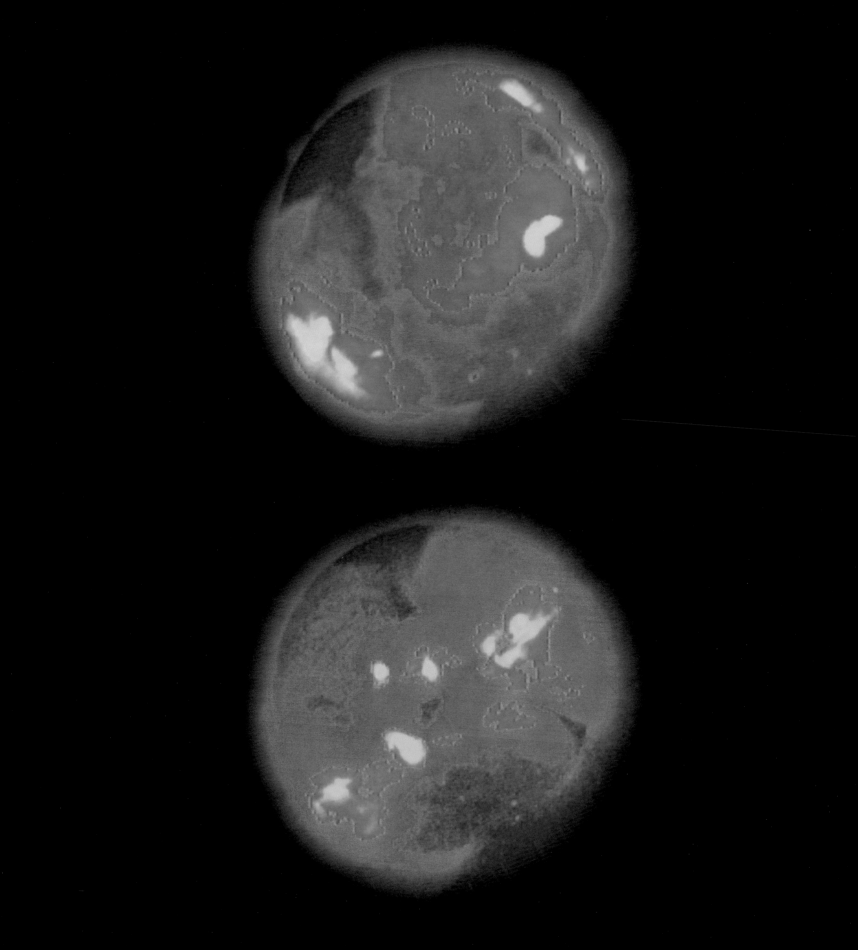

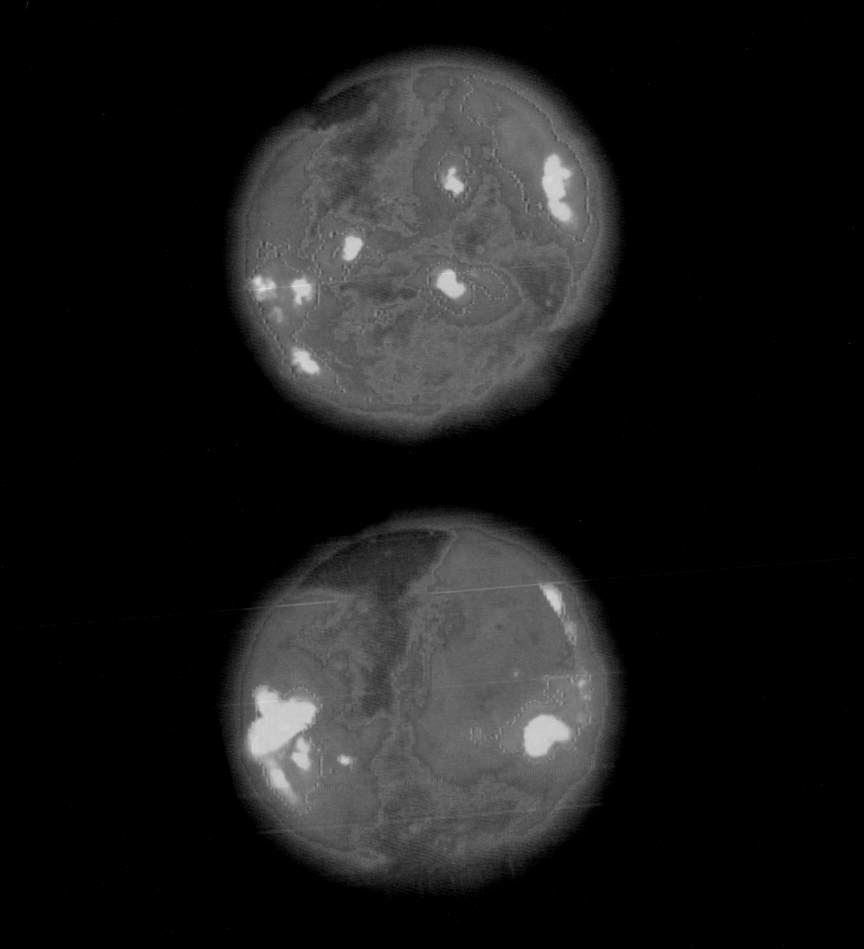

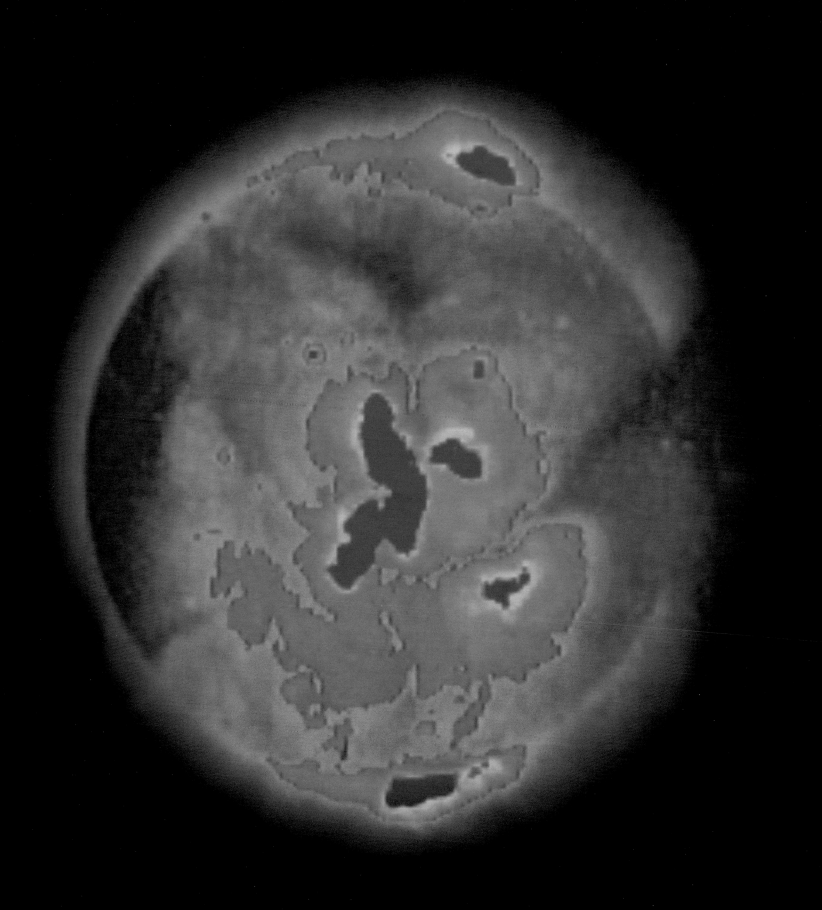

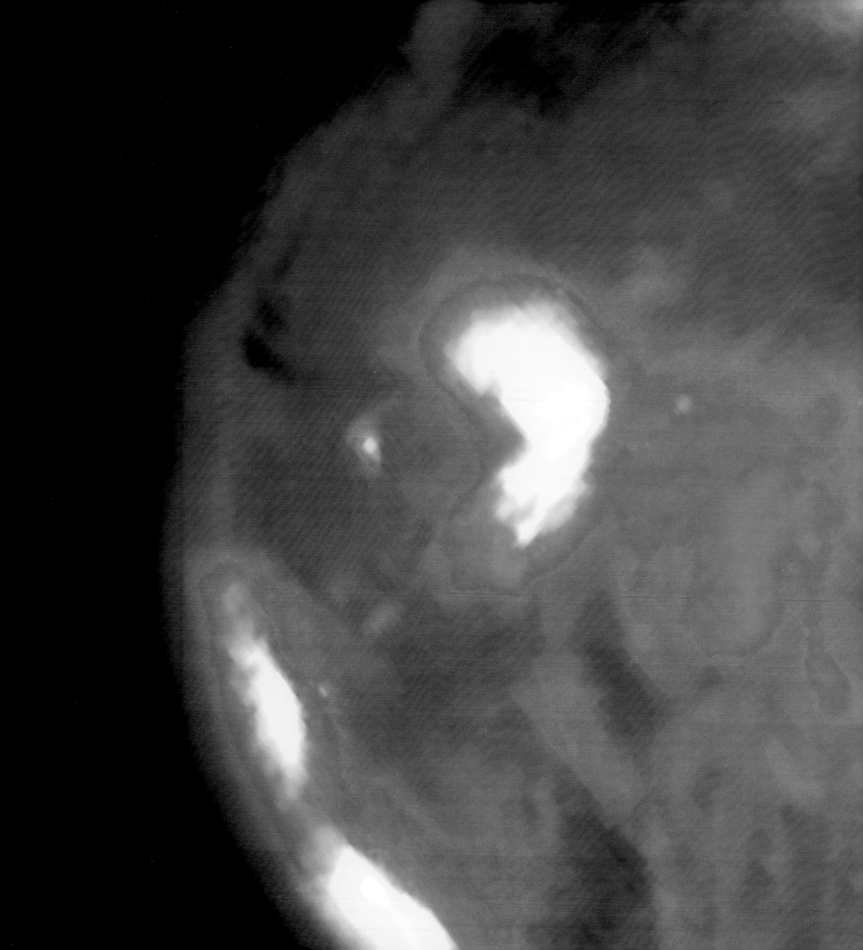

EUROPA

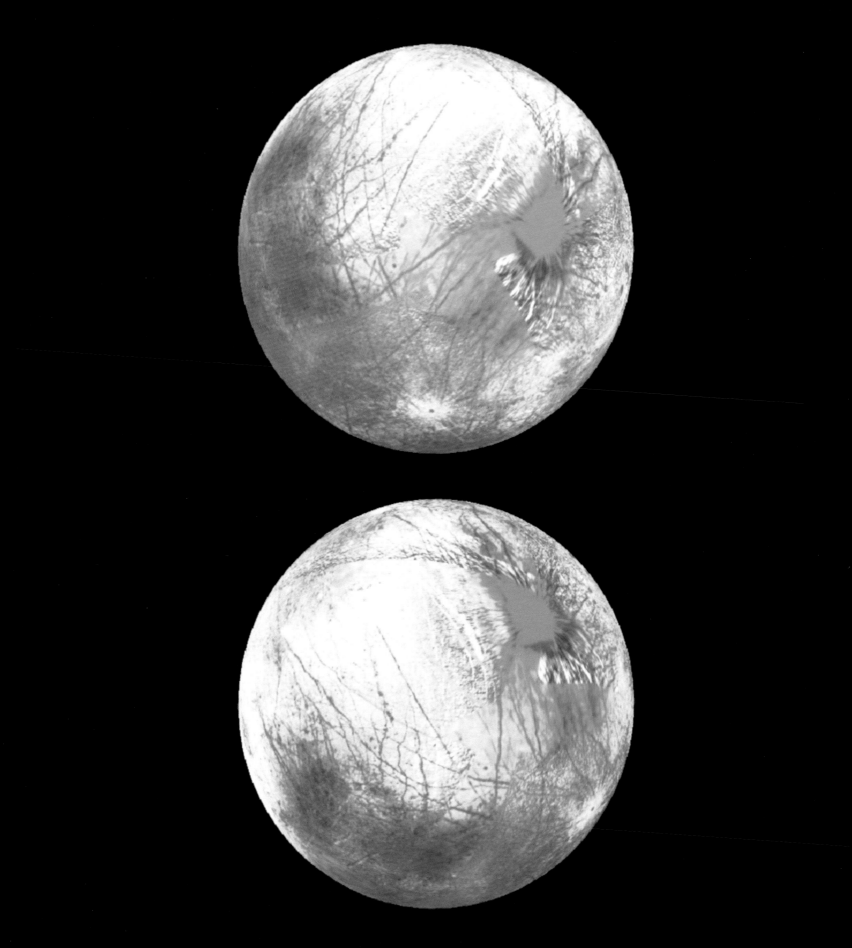

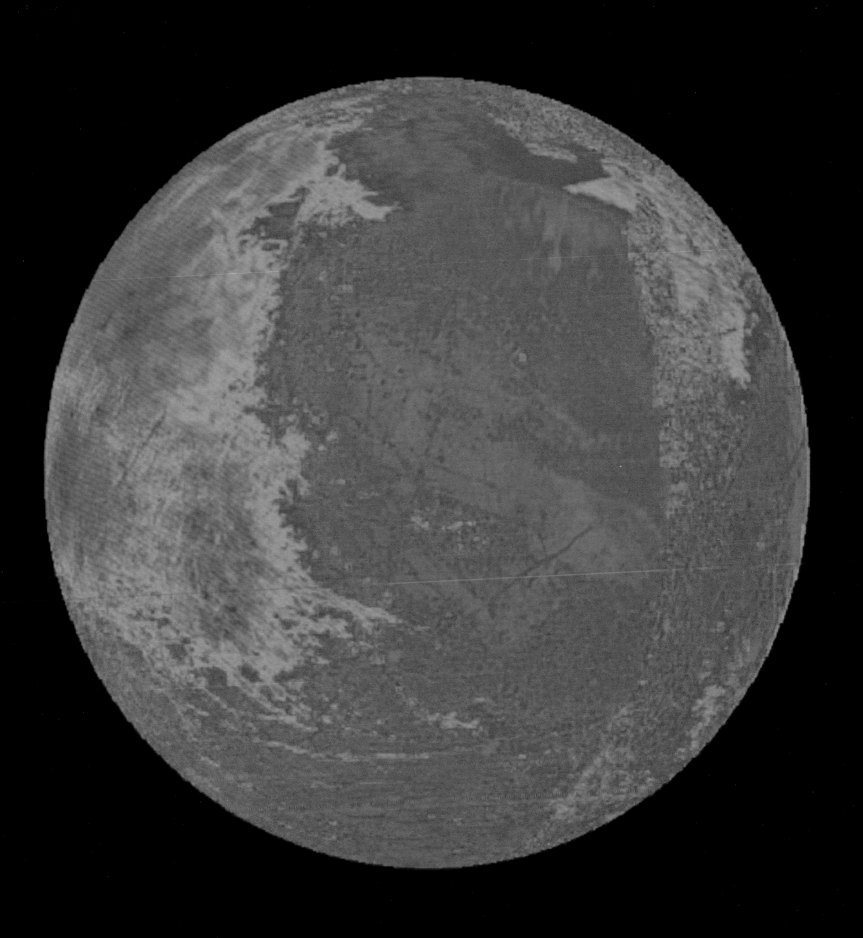

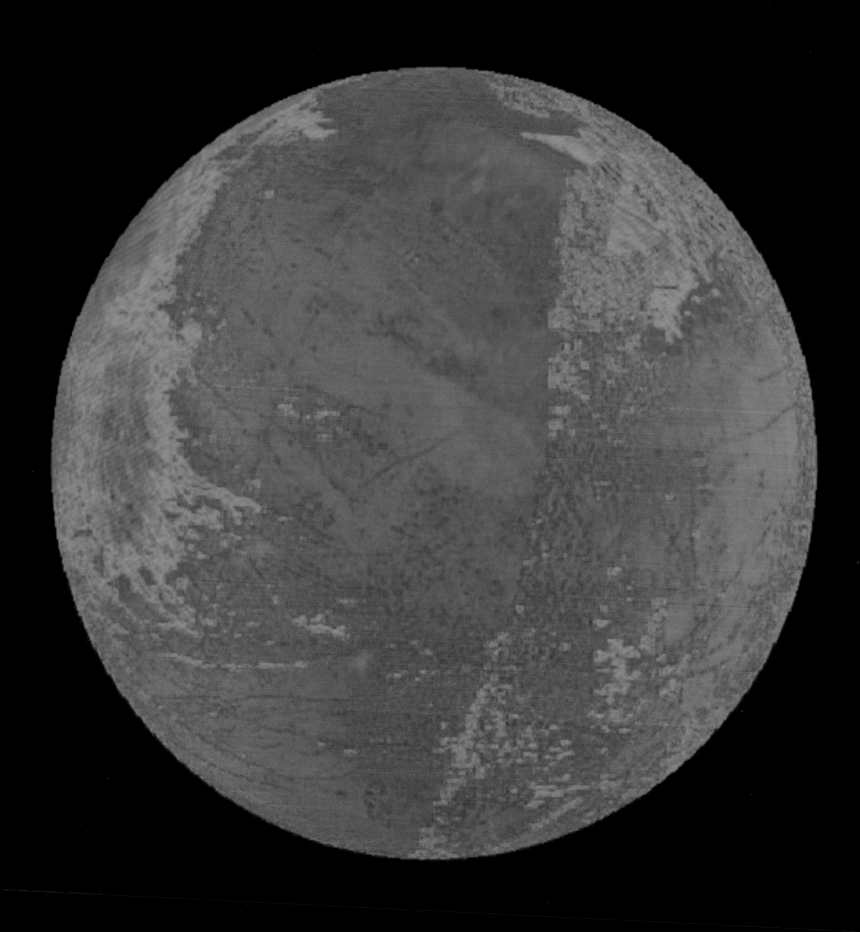

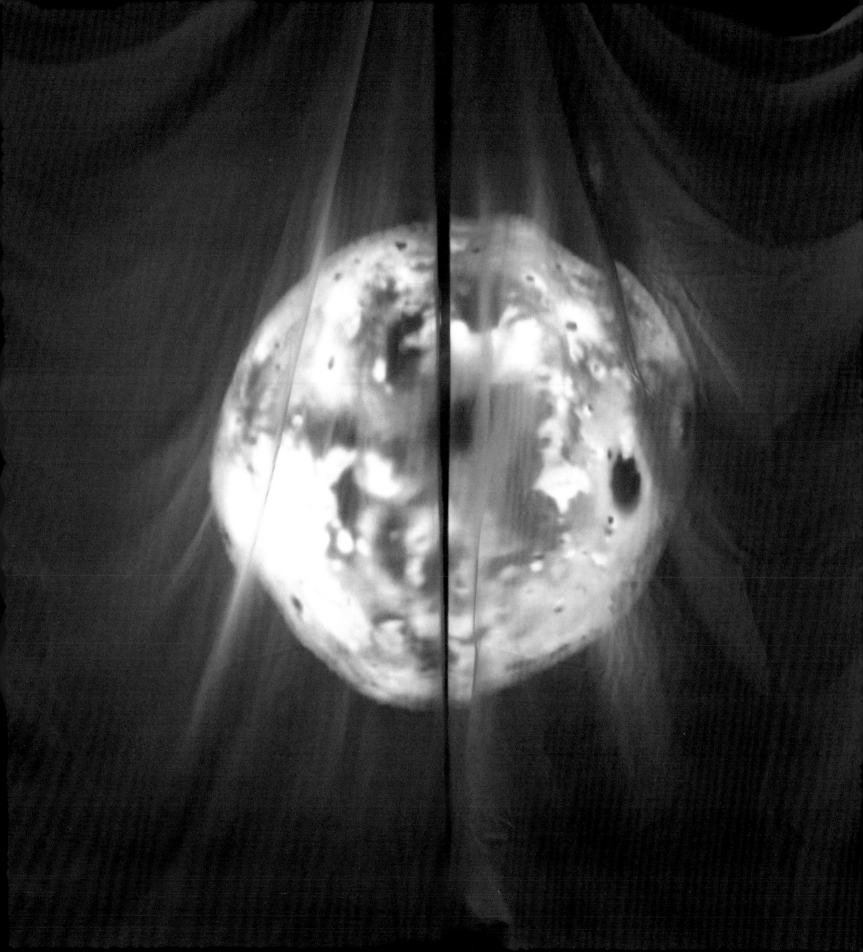

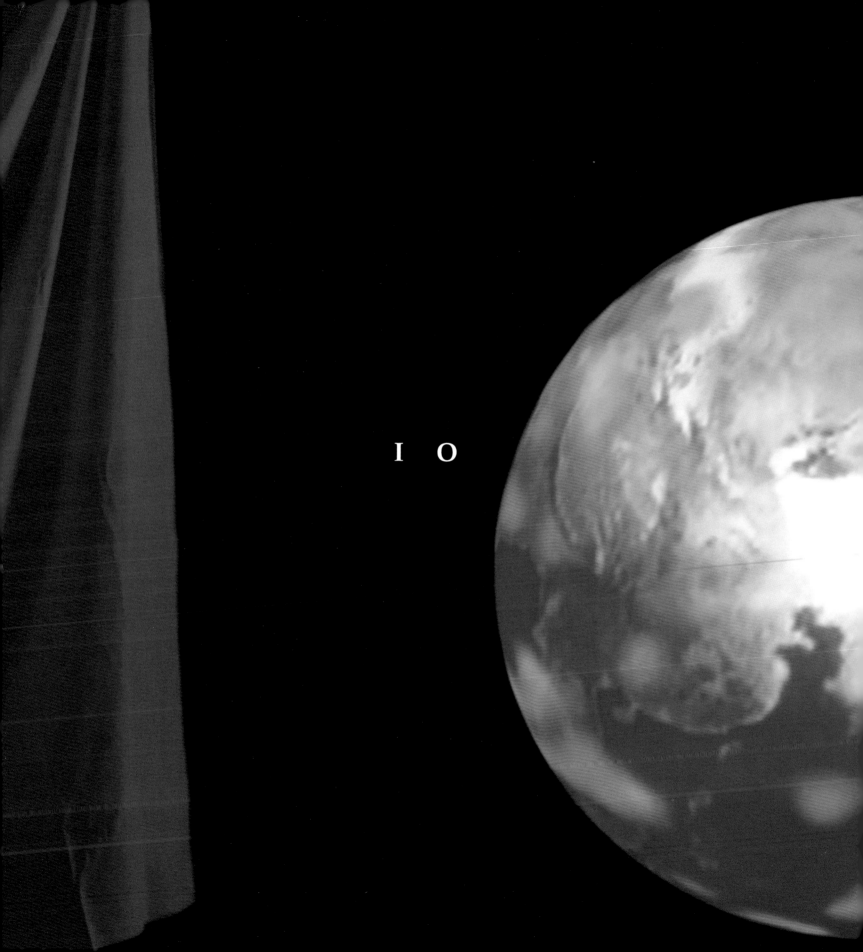

I O

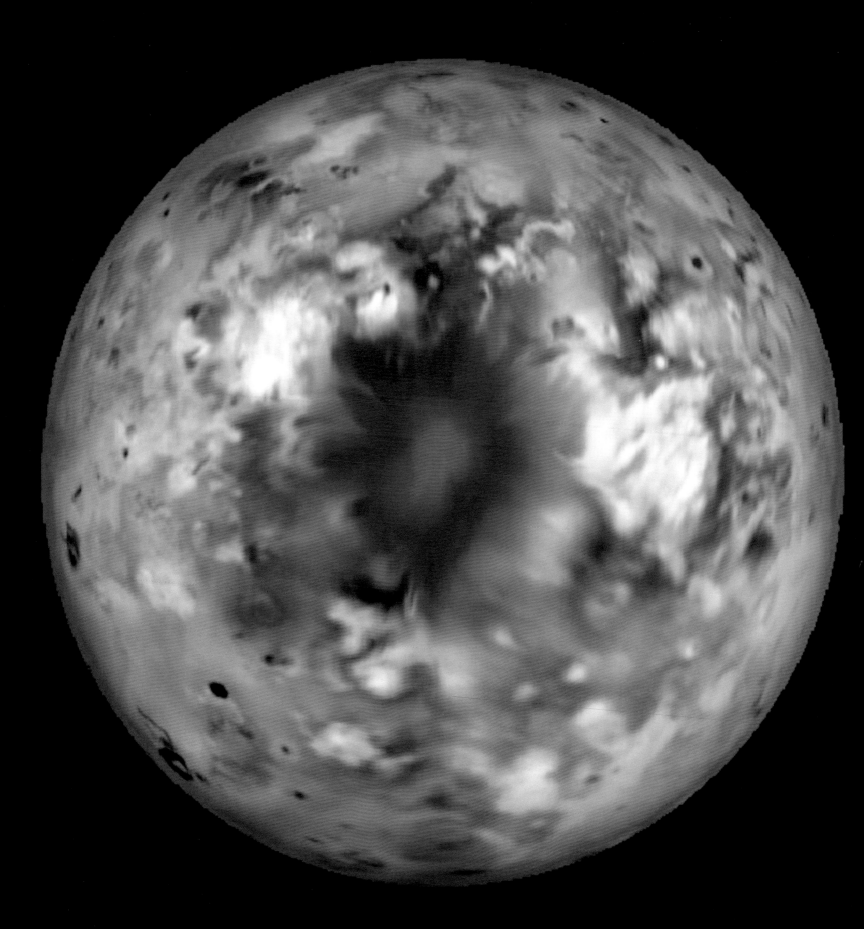

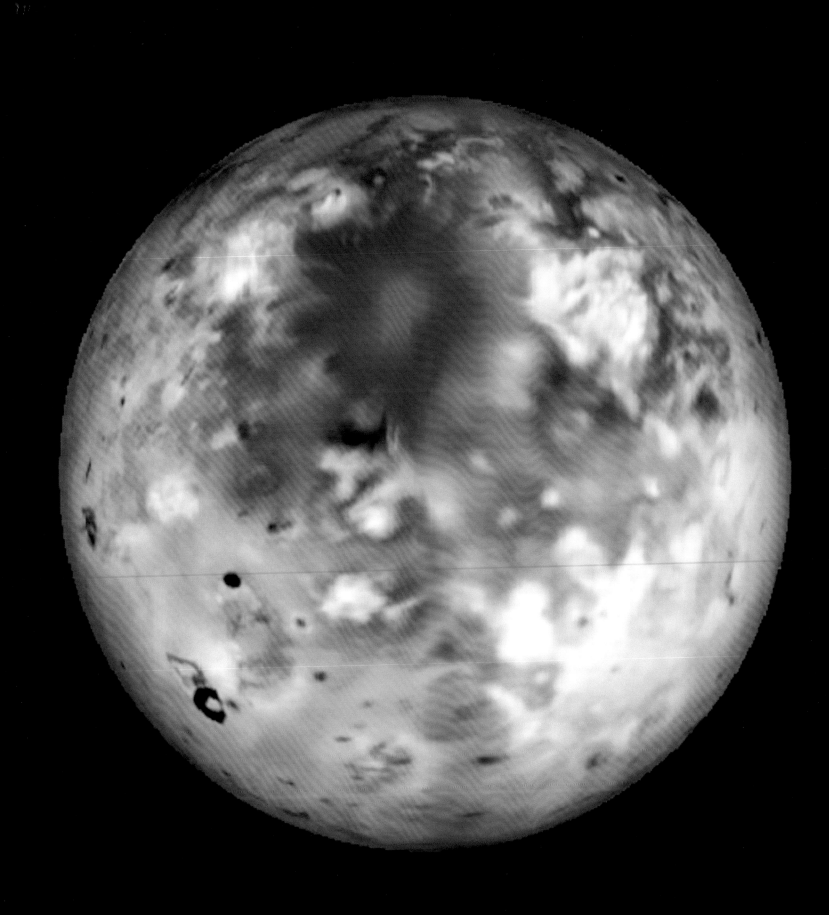

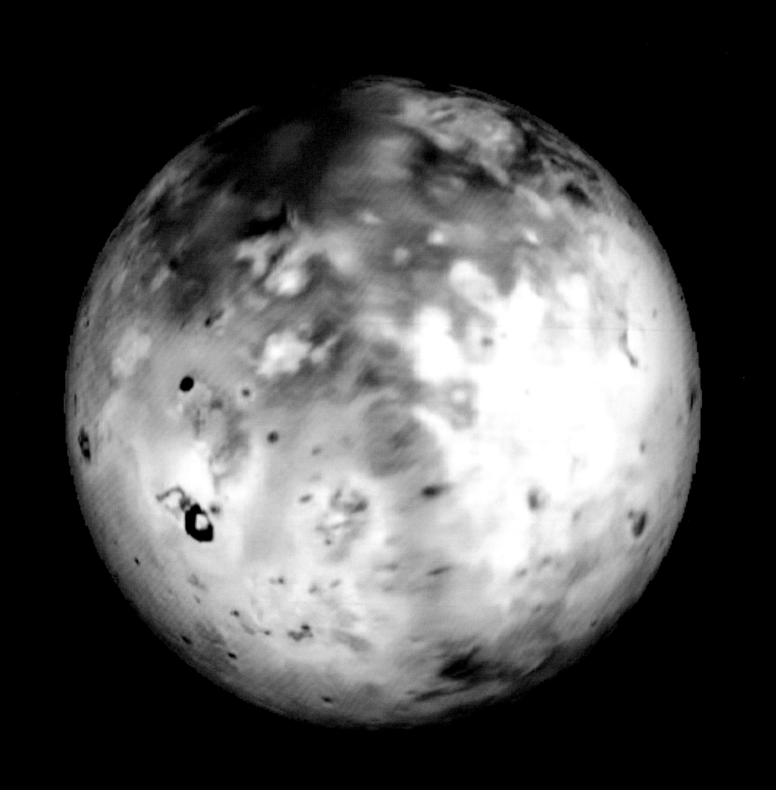

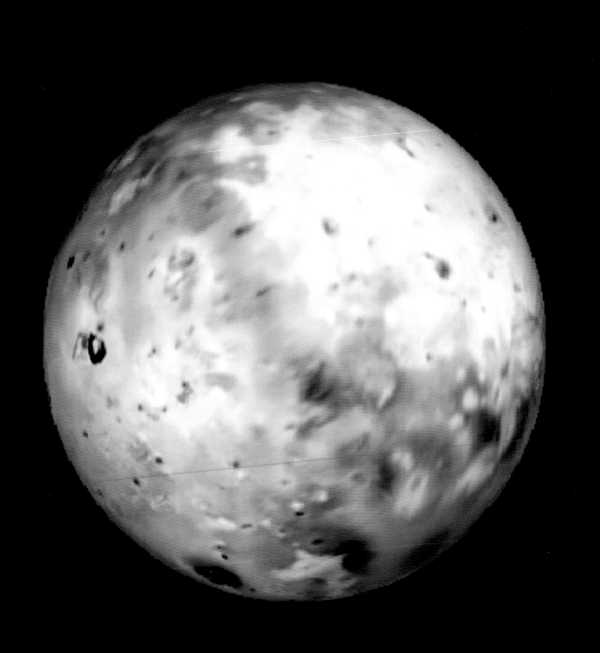

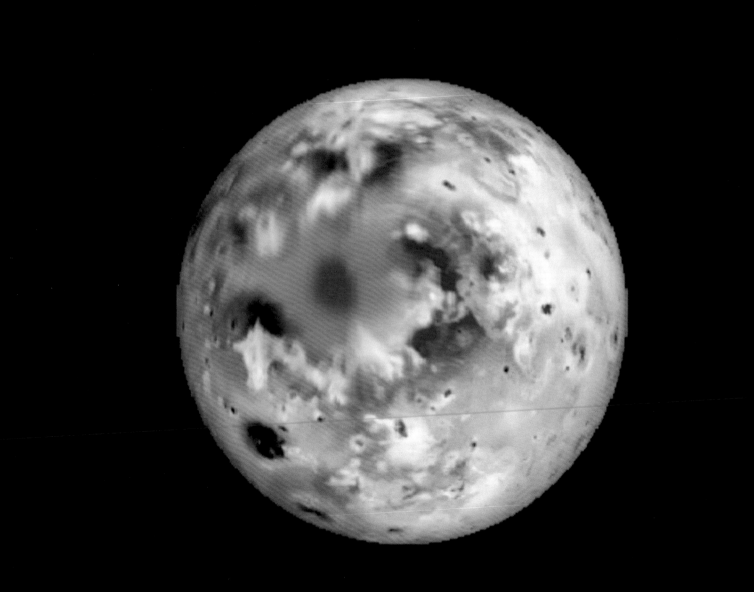

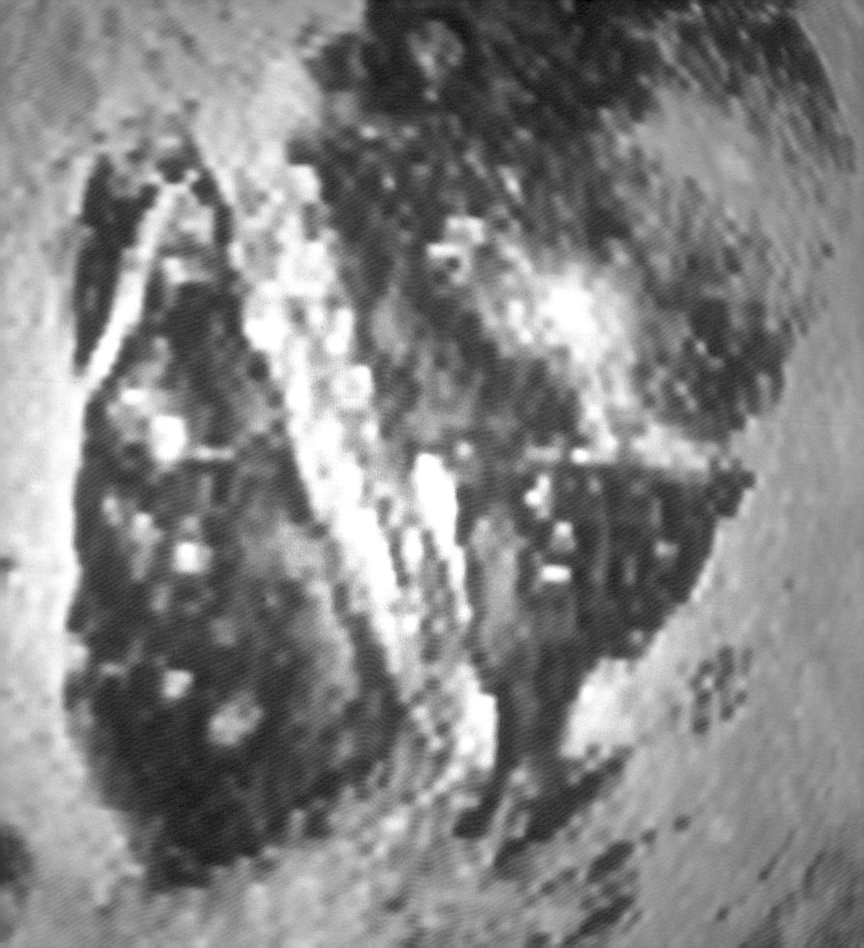

GANYMEDE

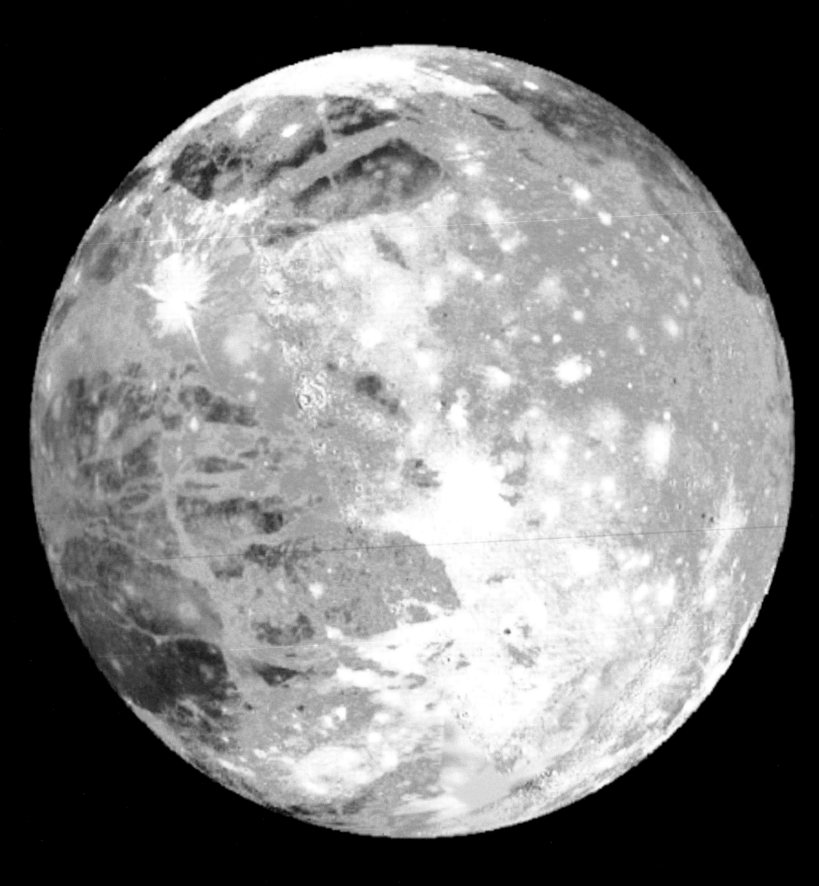

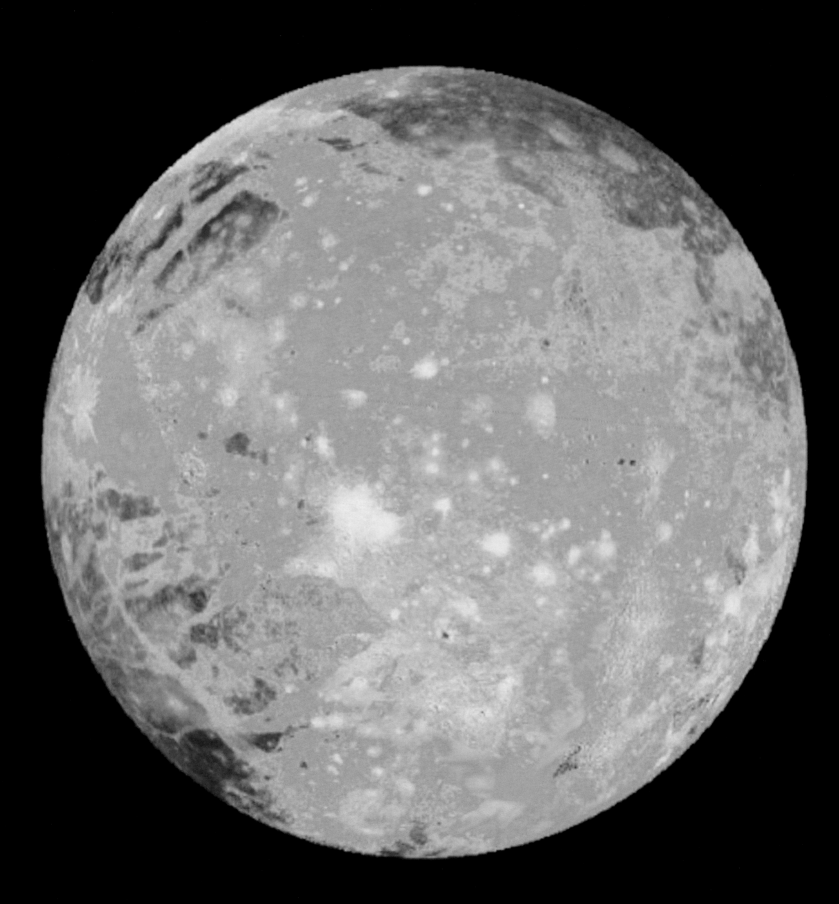

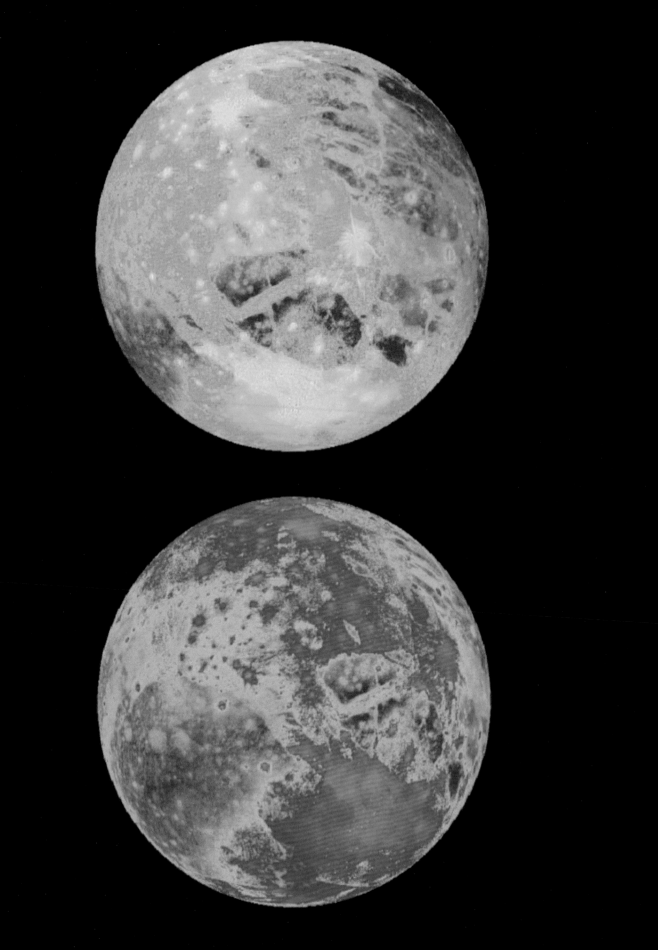

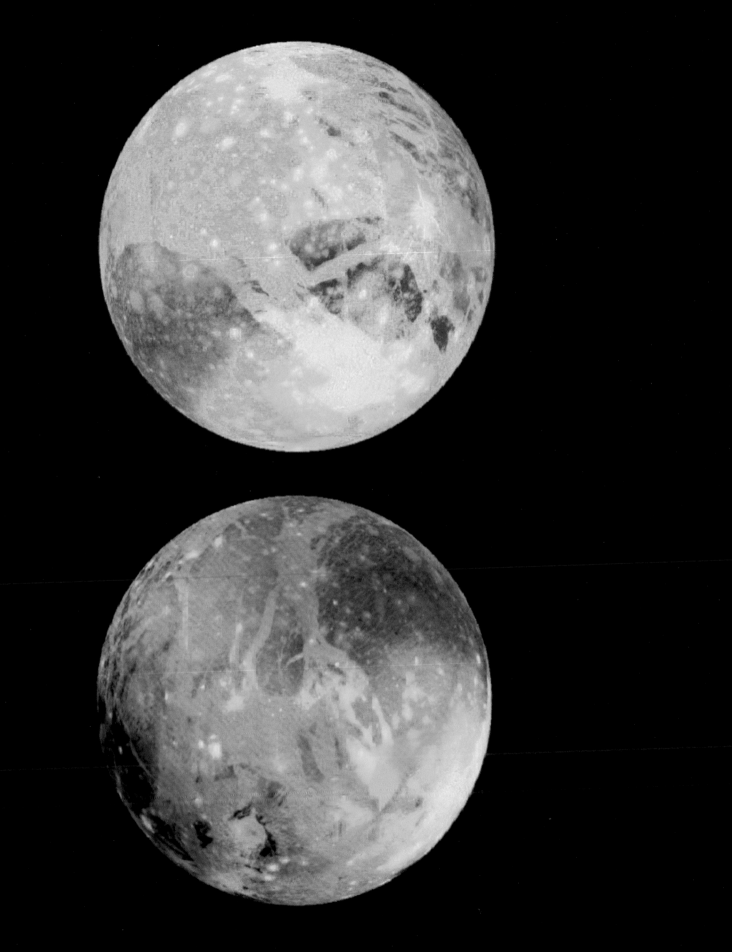

EARTH

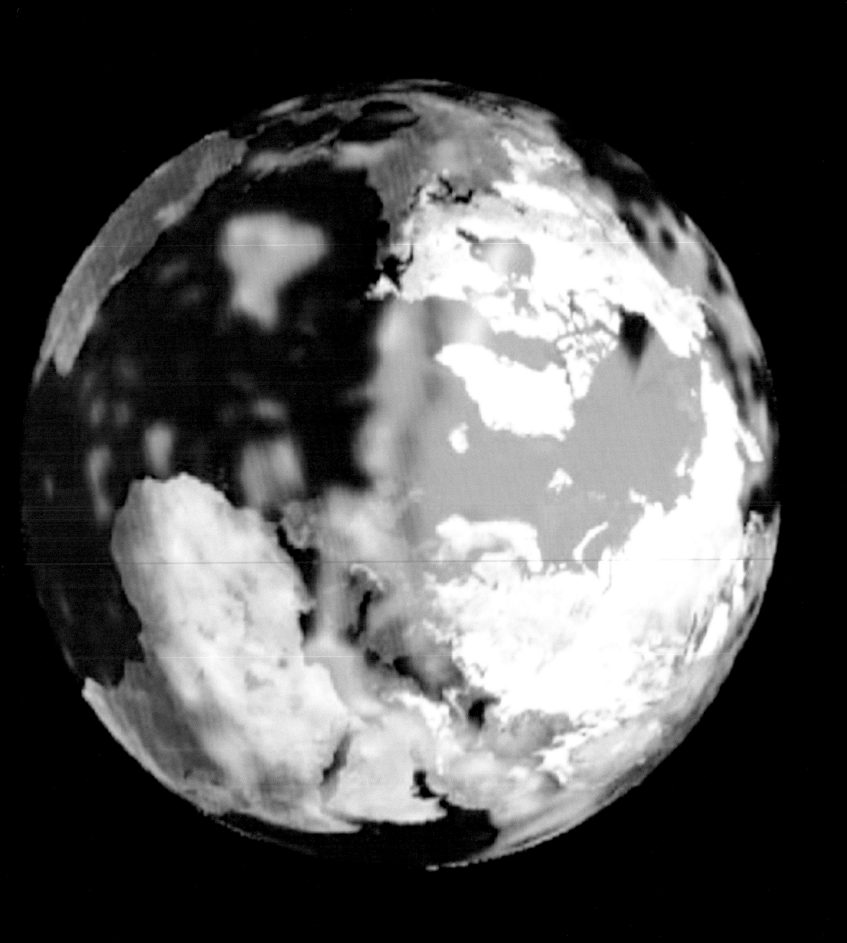

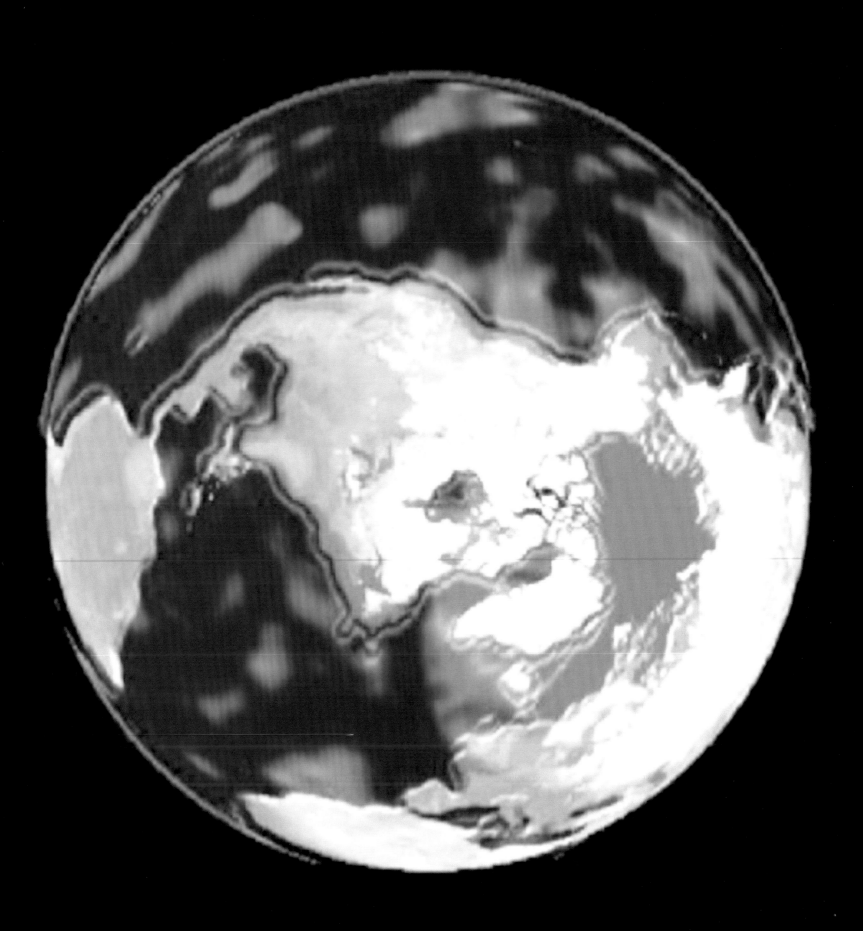

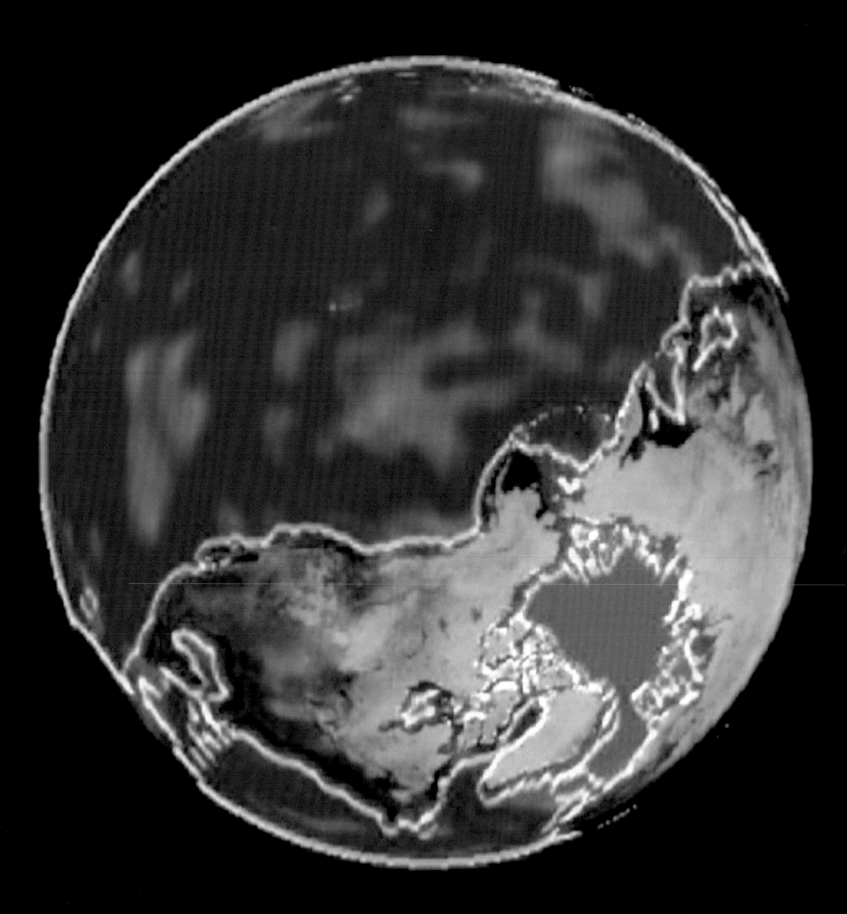

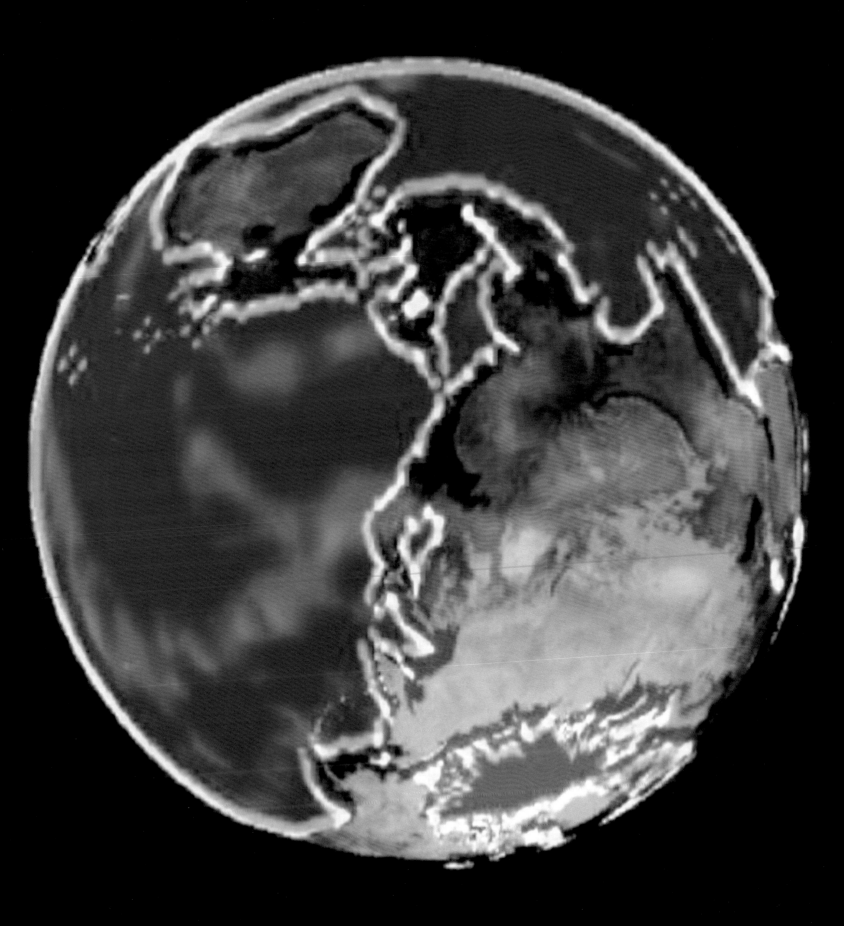

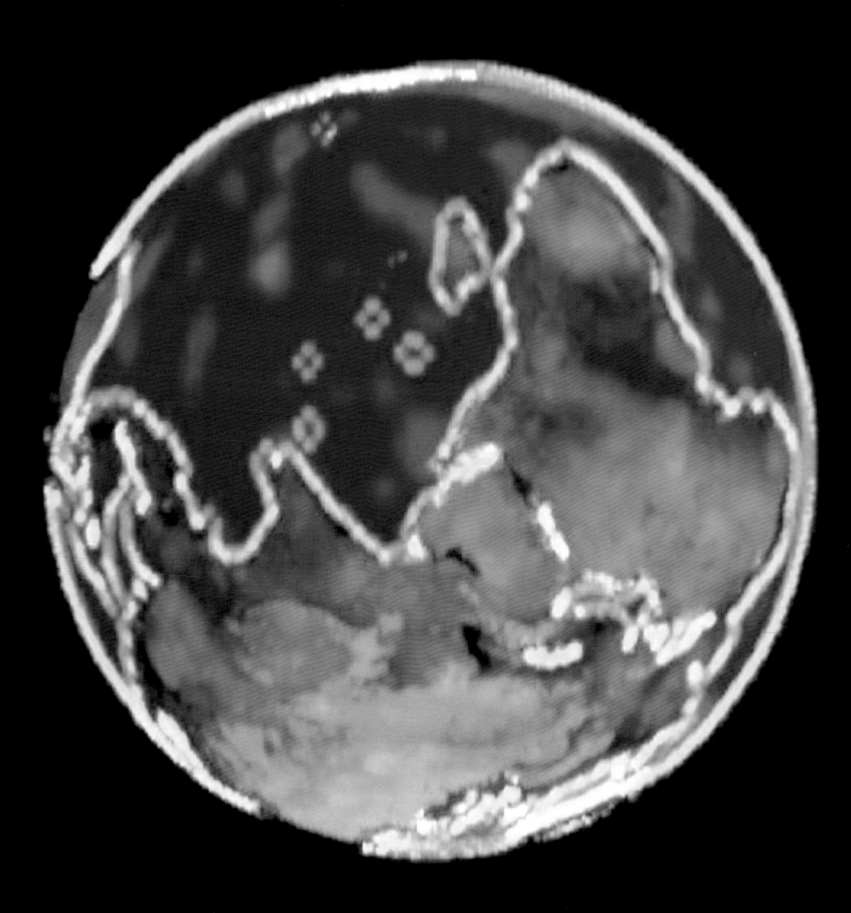

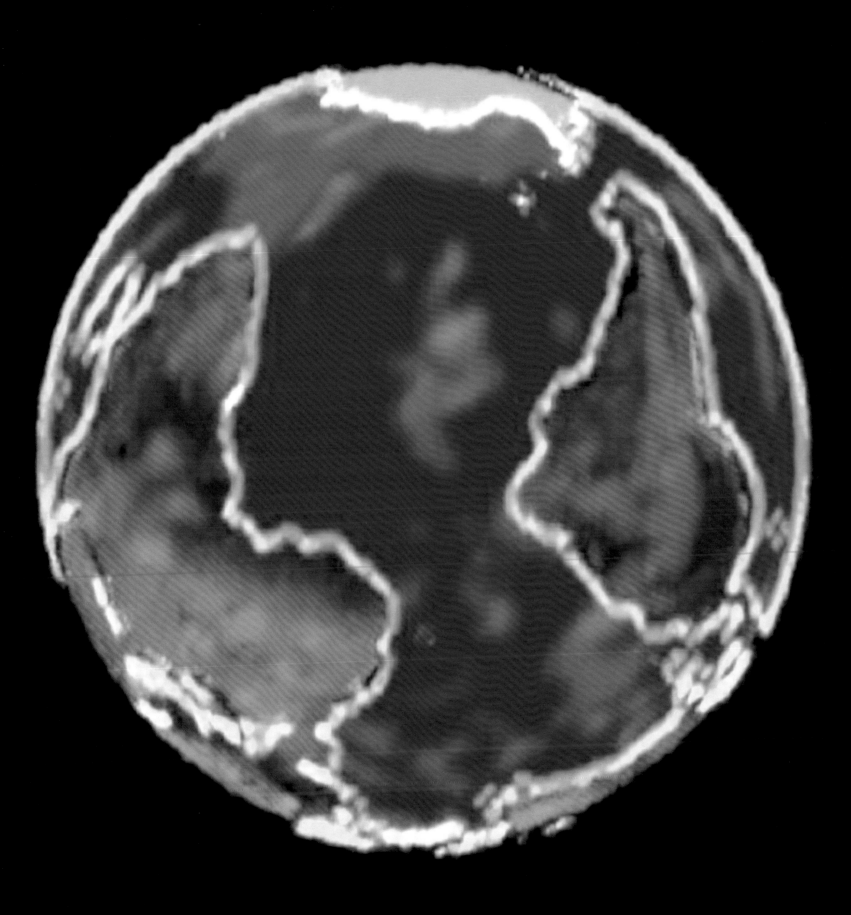

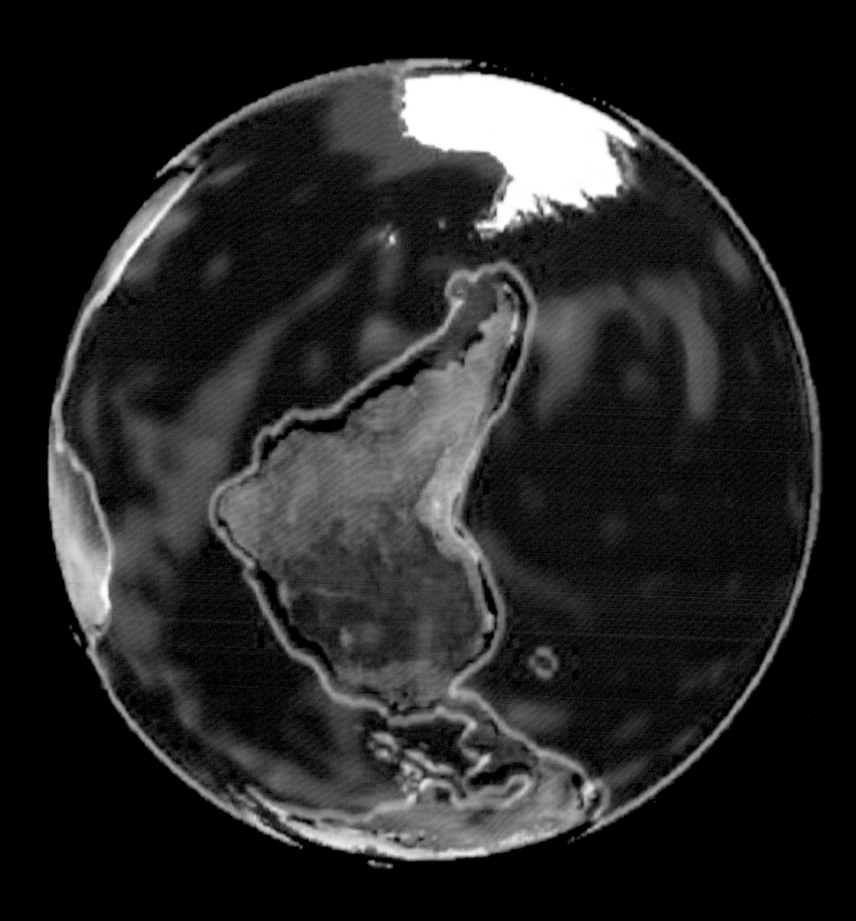

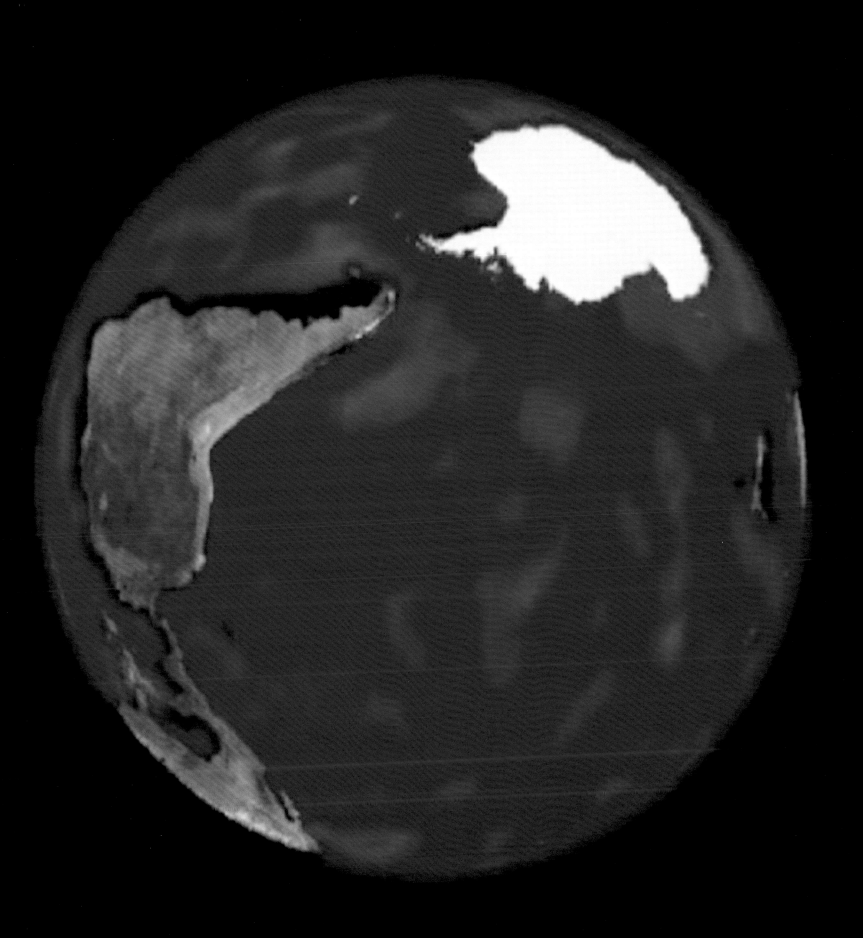

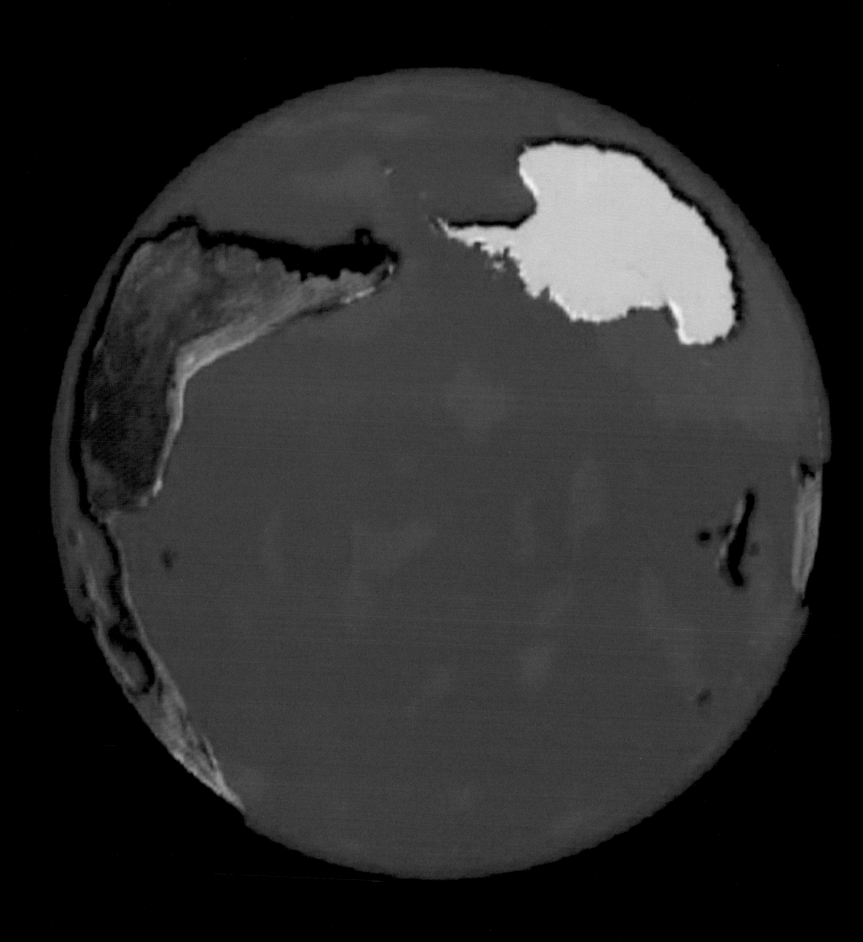

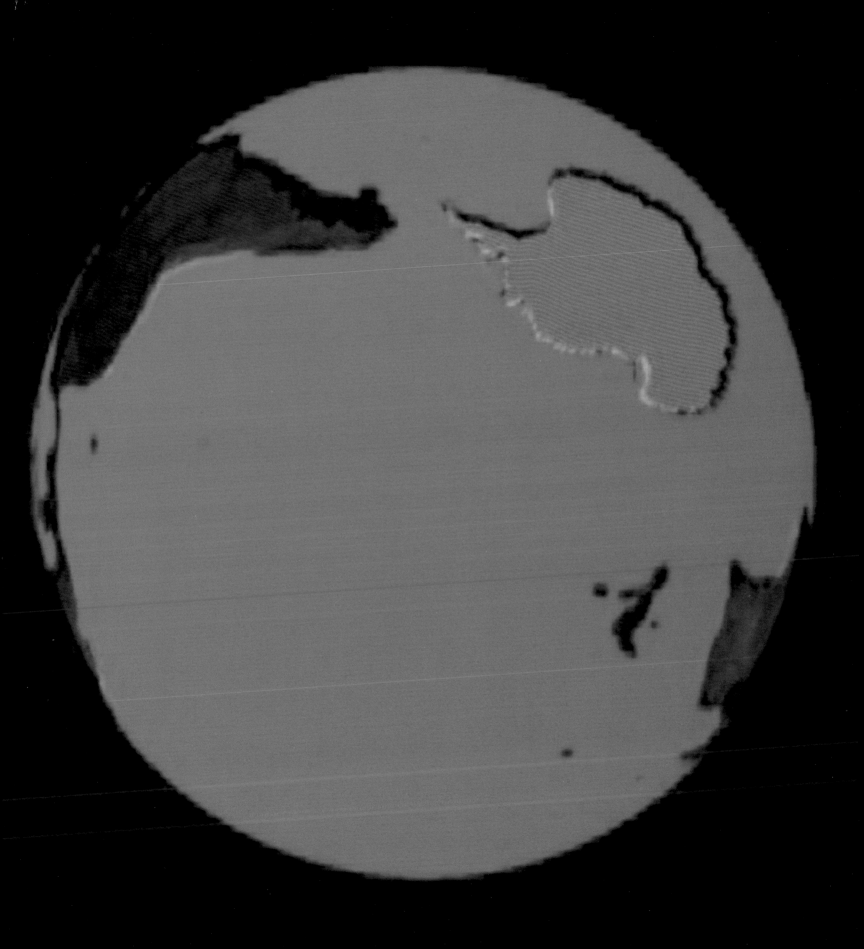

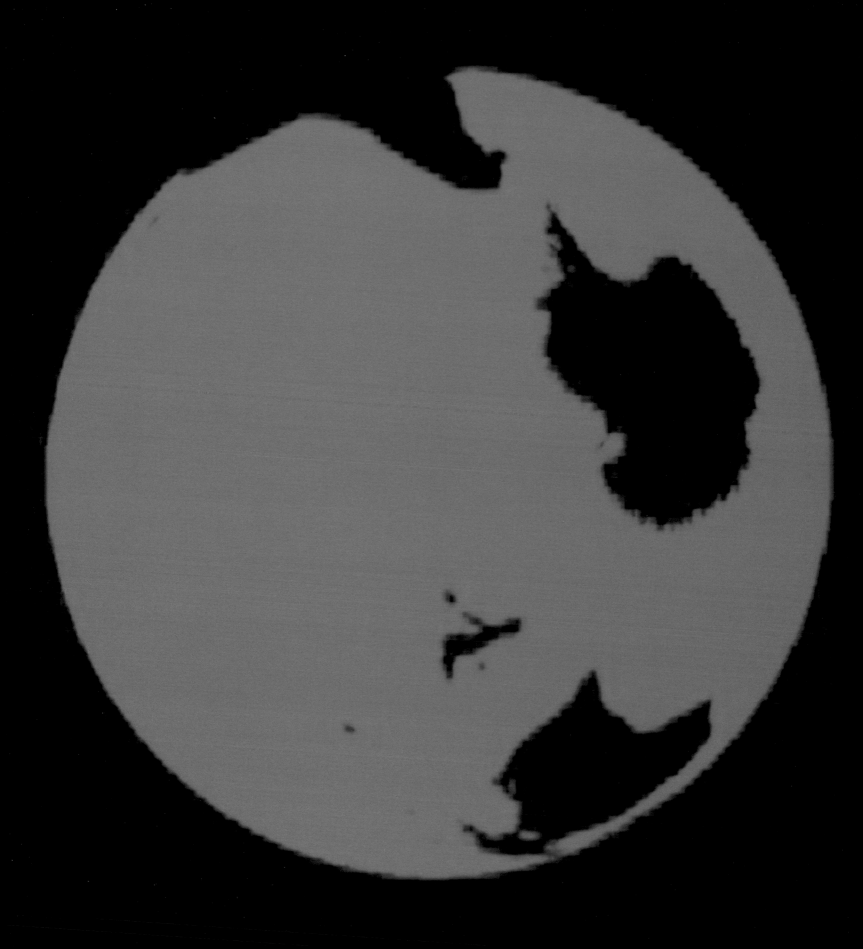

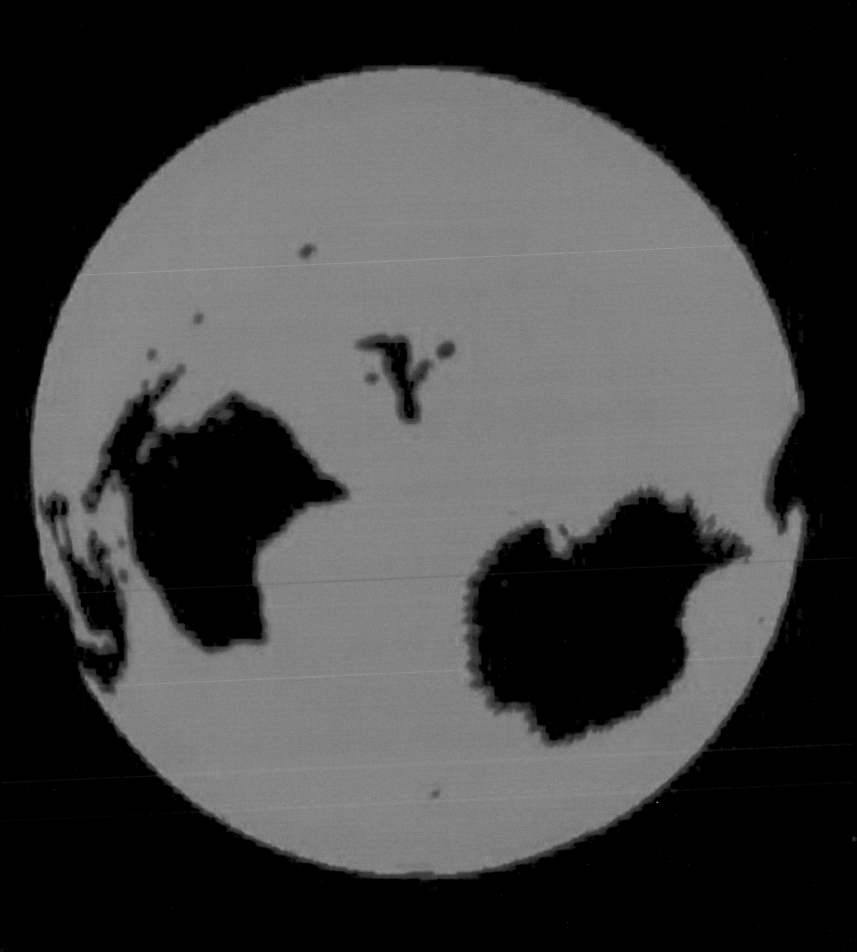

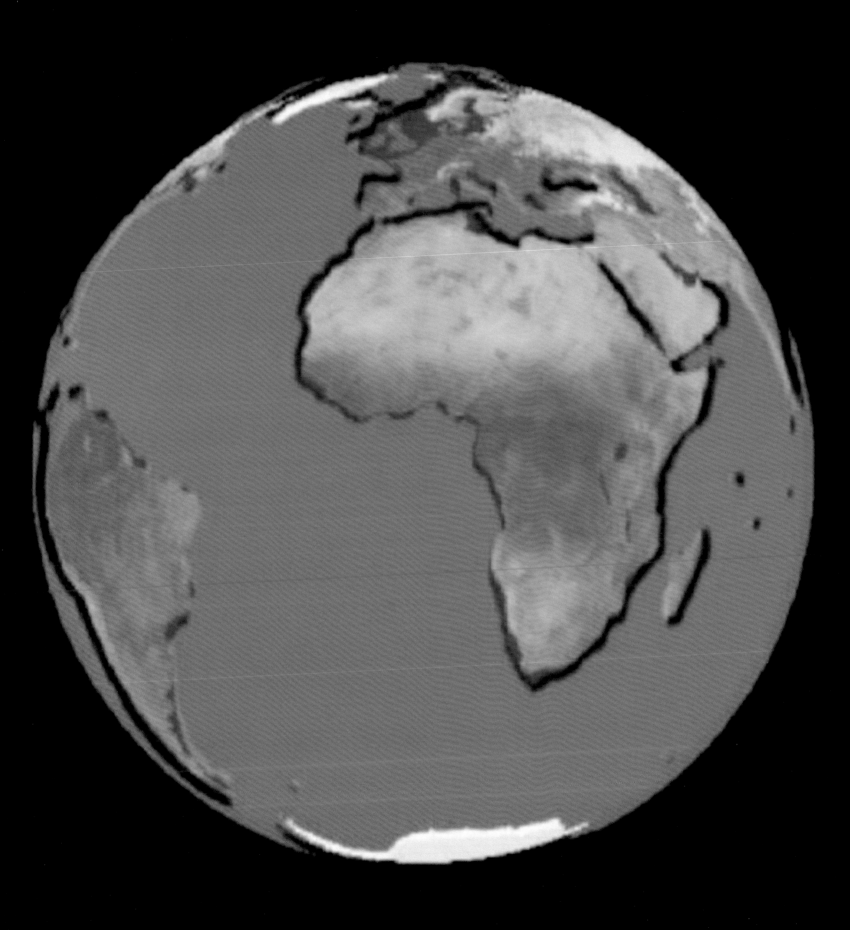

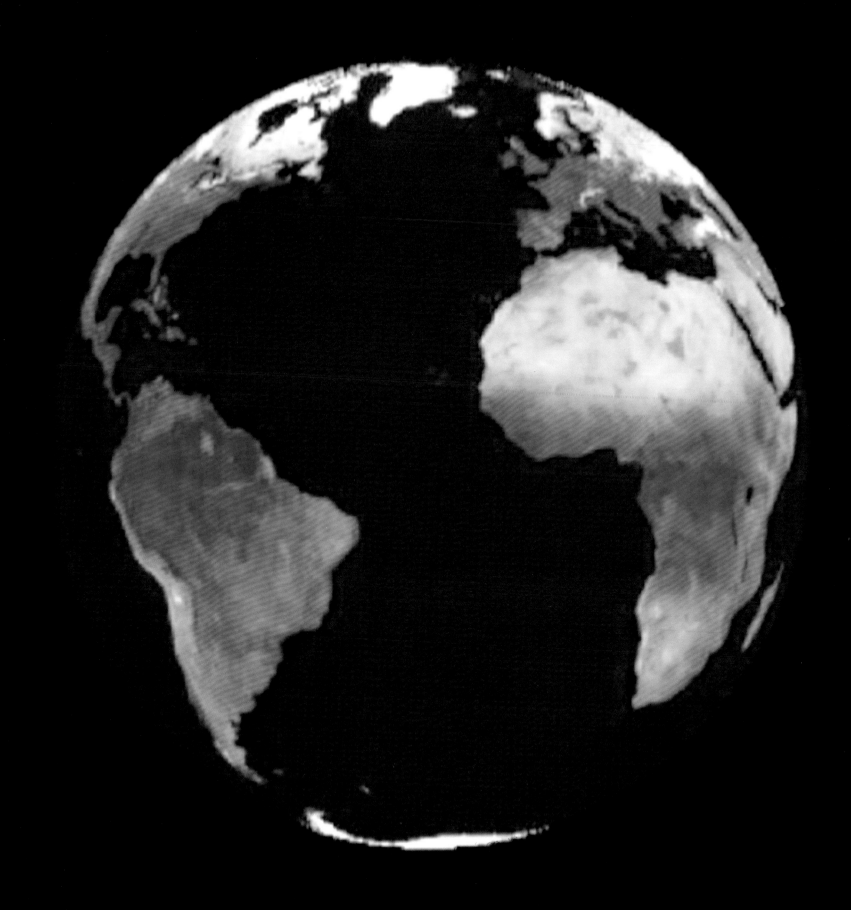

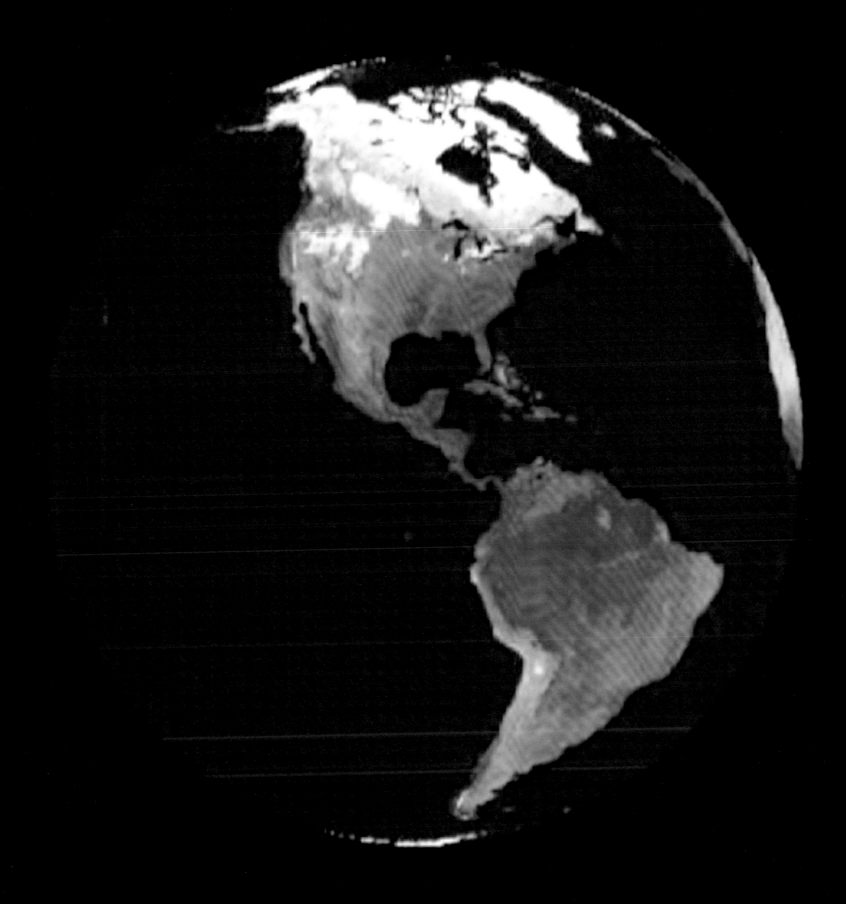

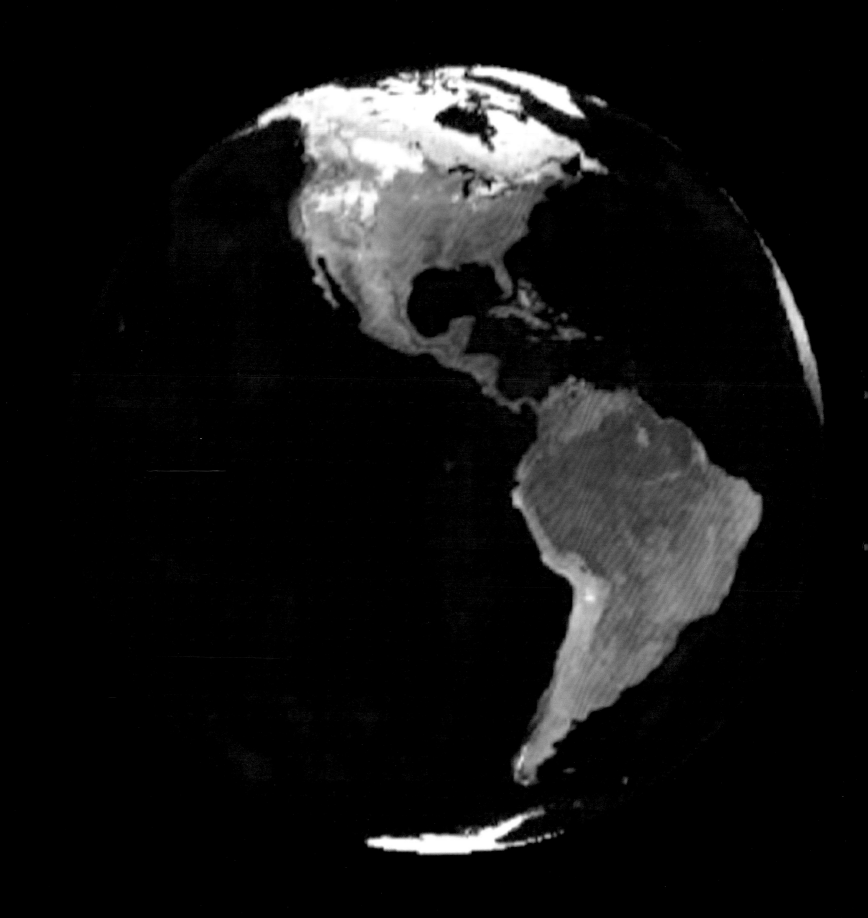

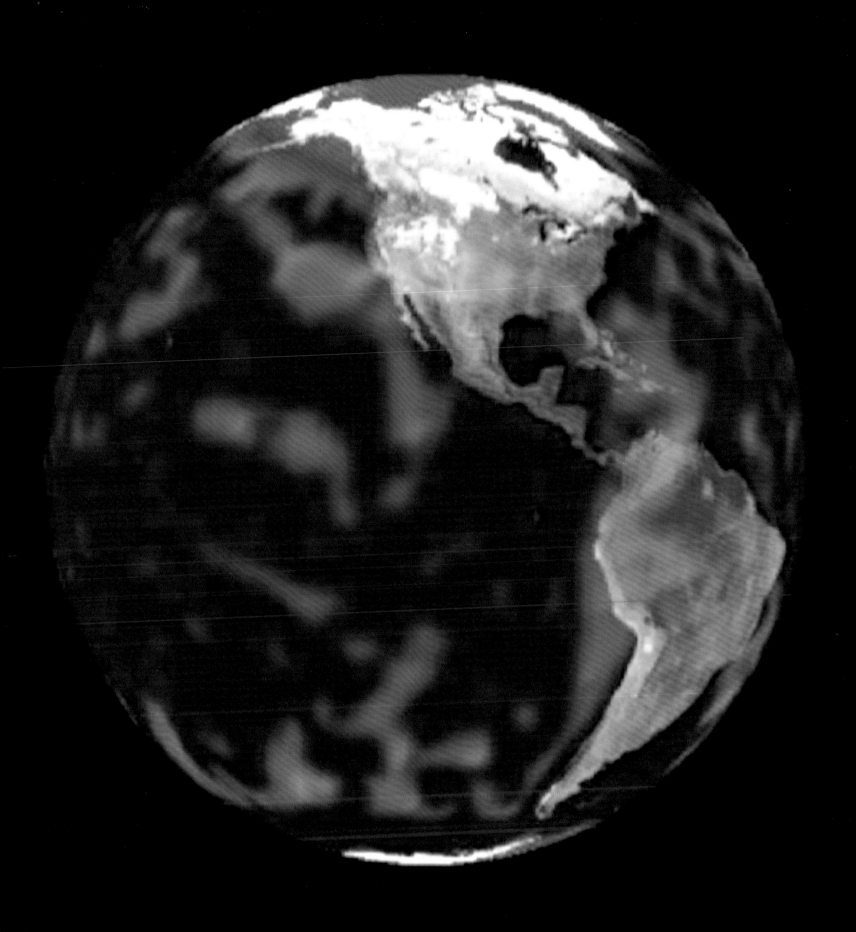

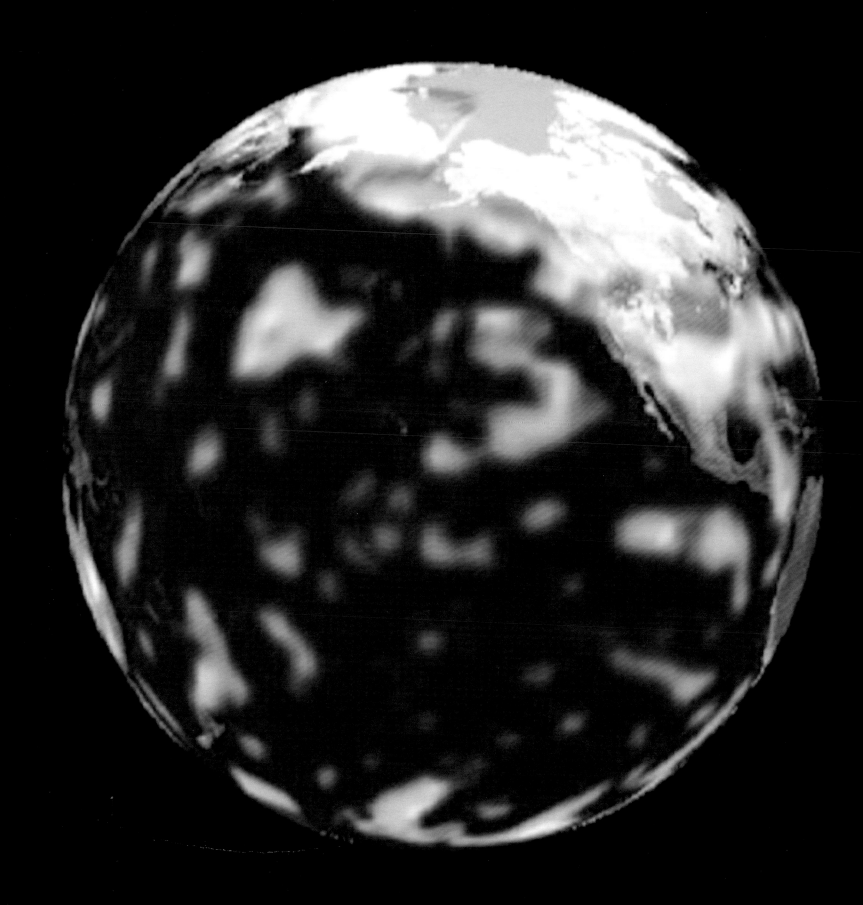

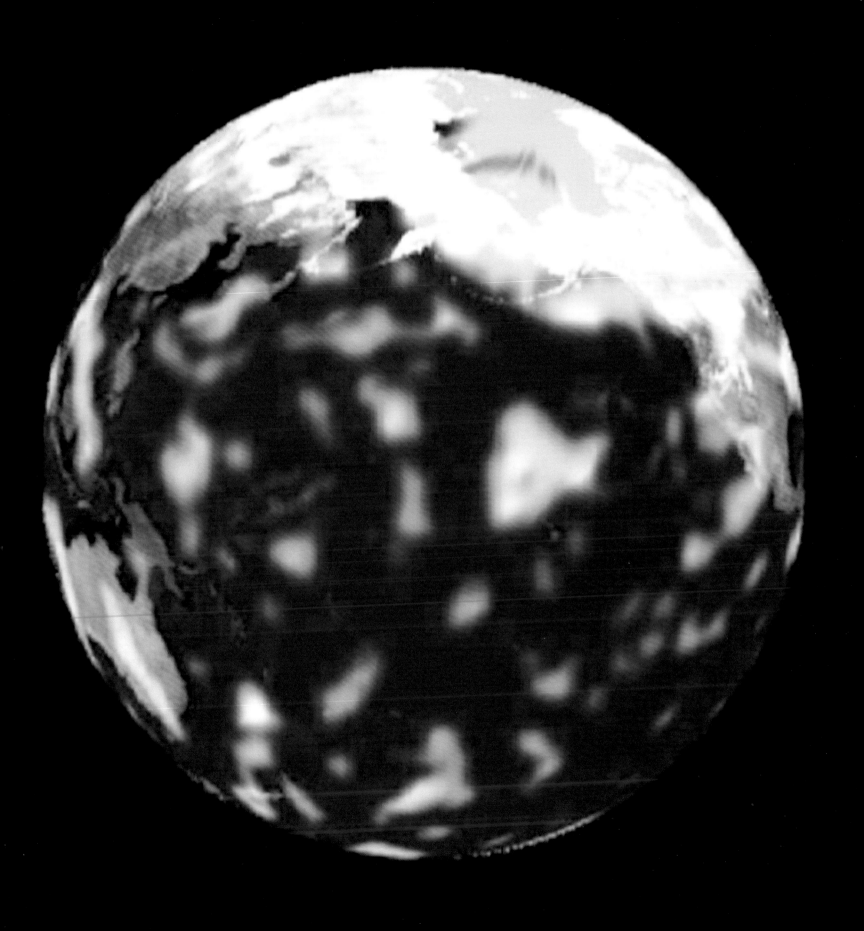

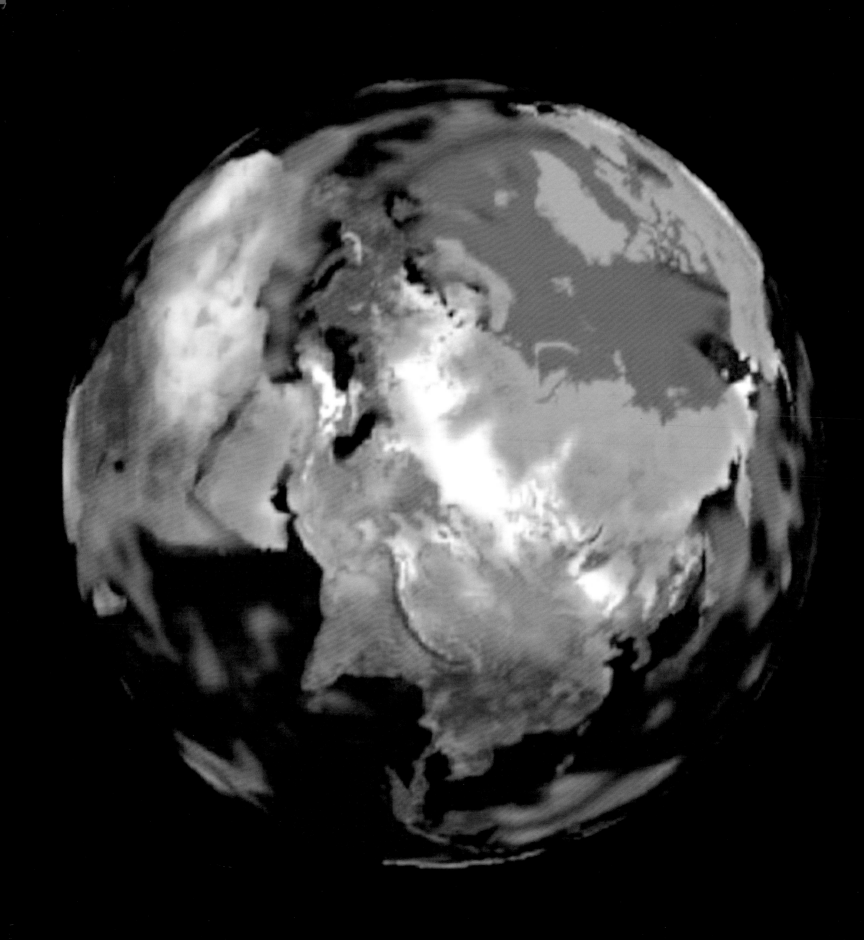

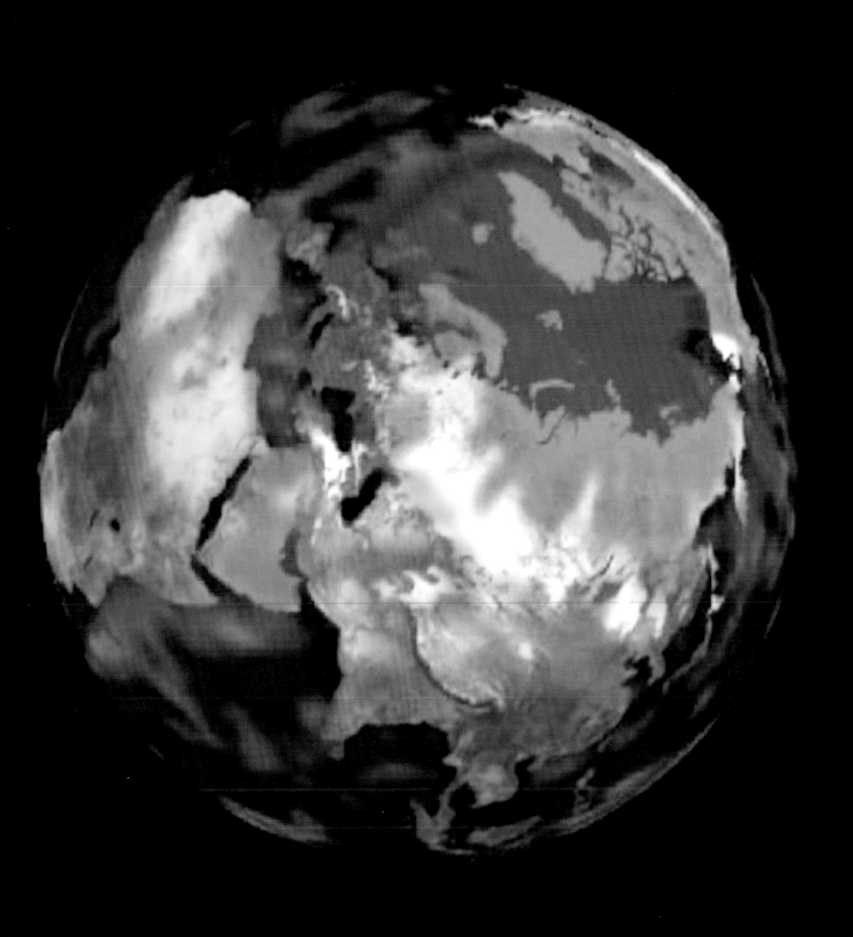

LIST OF WORKS IN EXHIBITION

SUN

2007
cloth with random digital video projection
installation dimensions variable;
cloth approximately 10 feet x 10 feet

EUROPA

2006
plastic hemisphere with looped digital video projection
4 feet 6 inches diameter

IO

2007
cloth and looped digital video projection
installation dimensions variable;
cloth approximately 10 feet high
viewable from both sides

GANYMEDE

2006
plastic hemisphere with looped digital video projection
4 feet 6 inches diameter

EARTH

2006
plastic hemisphere with looped digital video projection
5 feet diameter

Outdoor installation, June 28–September 1, 2007

SUN

2007
cloth with random digital video projection
installation dimensions variable;
approximately 20 feet x 20 feet

ACKNOWLEDGMENTS

I would like to thank the following people: Julie Martin, for extraordinary help in all areas, Evan Raskob, collaborating computer technician, Walter Smith, moon architect, and Susan Welchman, for her advice.

– R.W.

Source credits

Europa, Io, Ganymede, Earth; Digital source material from NASA.

Sun (indoor and outdoor installations); The solar X-ray images are from the Yohkoh
mission of ISAS, Japan. The X-ray telescope was prepared by the Lockheed-Martin
Solar and Astrophysics Laboratory, the National Astronomical Observatory of Japan,
and the University of Tokyo with the support of NASA and ISAS.

Photography credits

Benjamin Bloom: p. 6
Genevieve Hanson: p. 9; section dividers *Europa, Io, Ganymede, Earth*
Babette Mangolte: p. 11
© Robert R. McElroy/Licensed by VAGA, New York, NY: pp. 5, 8, 10
Evan Raskob: front and back cover; 5th, 6th, and 11th images in the *Europa* section

Design

Tomo Makiura

Production

Paul Pollard
Tucker Capparell

Printing

Meridian Printing, East Greenwich, Rhode Island

Library of Congress Control Number: 2007934939
ISBN: 978-1-930743-78-6